I0741008

Best of Books By the Bed #1

What Writers Are Reading Before Lights Out

Edited by Cheryl Olsen and Eric Olsen

BRIGHTCITYBOOKS
www.brightcitybooks.com

ISBN: 978-0-9795898-7-4

Edited by Cheryl Olsen and Eric Olsen
Cover design by Bill Girsch

Thanks!

We are enormously indebted to the generosity of the contributors herein, as well as to writers everywhere whose love of language and words and their purposeful arrangement on the page enrich all our lives.

Books and their methods of dissemination may change, but readers will continue to seek them out, to plumb their depths, and to share their myriad contents. And that, friends, is what this book is all about.

CONTENTS

Introduction

Whether they cover every inch of shelf space and every available flat surface or reside pristinely in an e-reader, books by the bed are the constant—and ever-changing—companions of avid readers and writers. They're often special, different from the tomes of daylight, flirtatious, fun, provocative friends we array within easy reach, our last contacts with the conscious world before we surrender to sleep, perchance to dream, and perchance to dream about what we just read....

The sampling of those books here is the first of an anticipated annual collection of guest posts from the *We Wanted to Be Writers* blog. Twenty-five writers share their personal stashes—nearly 250 books—and what earned these bedside status.

Eight of our contributors here are also featured in *We Wanted to Be Writers*. When doing the interviews for that book, we asked what books writers happened to have by the bed at that time. We sprinkled those fascinating lists in little boxes throughout the text. When we launched our website, http://wewantedtobewriters.com, we posted some of the original lists from the book. And then we invited visitors to the site to submit the books by *their* beds. This feature turned out to be quite popular, and evolved into a weekly series.

Some of the lists in this collection have been revised and updated since they were first posted, and in some cases they've been expanded to include more information about the books mentioned. There are a third more non-fiction than fiction titles here, plus a smattering of poetry, and incredibly, only one book with vampires in it, *The Historian,* by Elizabeth Kostova, and that's by the bed of this collection's co-editor, Eric Olsen. But he can explain!

In one appendix, we include a list of books written by our contributors, and in another, all the books they mention, arranged alphabetically by author.

We heartily condone the voyeuristic pleasures of others' reads and would love to know what's by your bed. Please drop by http://wewantedtobewriters.com and add your list to the comment box.

JEFFREY ABRAHAMS

Jeffrey Abrahams was born and grew up in Ohio, where he graduated from Miami University, Oxford. He earned an MFA in poetry from the University of Iowa Writers' Workshop in 1977.

He has worked as a journalist (staff writer for the *Los Angeles Times* and *Oakland Tribune*) and freelance writer, and currently serves as a consultant and copywriter in communications, marketing and advertising in San Francisco.

In addition to publishing poems, short stories, magazine articles, and newspaper columns, he is the author of *The Mission Statement Book: 301 Corporate Mission Statements from America's Top Companies*, now in its third edition. Jeffrey is also an enthusiastic salsa dancer.

I'm currently on an art and art history jag along with a non-stop photography obsession. And I go to a lot of auctions. So my bedside book list looks like this:

Lynn H. Nicholas, *The Rape of Europa: The Fate of Europe's Treasures in the Third Reich and the Second World War*. Fascinating story. A compelling read. A page-turner like a thriller, although we all know who-done-it. There's a terrific film version well worth seeing.

Dave Hickey, *Air Guitar: Essays on Art & Democracy*. Why isn't Dave Hickey a household name? His prose is original, muscular, funny, and surprising. He connects dots in vectors unexplored. I read certain paragraphs over and over to revel in his voice.

Therese Mulligan and Hans-Michael Koetzle, *Photo Icons: The Story Behind the Pictures*. As a photography buff, I'm buried deep in books and ephemera (auction catalogs, monographs, and back issues of *Aperture Magazine*) to educate myself about the art and craft of making pictures. I love learning about the real stories behind famous shots. This book reveals so much of how magic, art, craft, and luck all dovetailed to produce famous images. A good follow-up to my reading is the brilliant *Looking at Photographs: 100 Pictures from the Collection of the Museum of Modern Art* by **John Szarkowski**, a survey of photography's evolution.

Nicholson Baker, *The Anthologist.* I like to ask people what they're reading. The owner of a small art gallery in San Francisco enthused about this book so I picked up a copy. What a hoot. A novel about a hapless fellow who is tasked with writing an introduction to a new anthology of rhyming poetry, but he's procrastinating with great verve and inventiveness. Very funny on every page. Baker clearly loves poetry (and knows his stuff) and he drops more names than you could pick up at a Writers' Workshop post-reading cocktail party.

The New Yorker. Various issues. I believe my subscription is paid up through 2018.

DOUG BORSOM

Doug Borsom grew up in Hinsdale, Illinois. He studied physics at Case Western Reserve University in Cleveland, but transferred to Knox College in Galesburg, Illinois to study literature, and discovered creative writing classes. He had started writing at age 12 because he thought books were powerful, so writing conferred power.

He completed his MFA in fiction from the University of Iowa Writers' Workshop in 1975. "I don't think of myself as a writer," he says. "It's just something I do." After Iowa, he taught creative writing for three years at Southwest Missouri

State before returning to school to study mathematics at the University of Wisconsin. For 20 years, his day job was in the computer industry. Doug lives in Pasadena and is writing a novel.

The more good short stories I read, the harder it is for me to remember why the novel is considered "better" or "more serious" or anything else other than simply longer and different. Then there are the nightstand ephemera, which flit through like the ectoplasmic insects in time-lapse segments of nature films, or *The New Yorker*. By my bed now:

Lucius Shepard, *The Jaguar Hunter*. A collection of stories. Some magical realism and Central American settings, a vein of *Apocalypse Now*. The comparison may be unfair to Shepard, but reading the stories that featured U.S. soldiers patrolling the jungles of Central America reminded me of just how very good Joe Haldeman [see page 26] is at writing about grunts.

Niall Ferguson, *The Ascent of Money: A Financial History of the World*. Interesting, popular history of finance, a subject not much discussed at the Workshop. Turns out that Lloyd Blankfein's antecedents can be traced back 5,000 years to Mesopotamia. And they thought they were too big to fail.

Franz Kafka, *The Collected Stories*. I would not want to live in Kafka's head, but visiting there is a good thing. A reminder of other ways of thinking and writing.

Clarence Darrow, *The Story of My Life*. Small town boy born a few years before the civil war, died just before World War II. Darrow saw the country transformed from a rural, agrarian culture, argued some of the great labor and criminal cases (defended Eugene Debs after the Pullman Strike, Leopold and Loeb, and Ossian Sweet), and likely bribed some jurors. Loved lost causes. Loved the underdog. Loved the spotlight.

David Ferry, translator, *The Odes of Horace*. What to say about the calming effect of a lyric voice two millennia old speaking directly to you? And immediately connecting?

Tobias Wolff, ed., *The Vintage Book of Contemporary American Short Stories*. Just a lot of fine short stories, many of them likely familiar to readers of *We Wanted to Be Writers*. When I'm dried up, a story like **Leonard Michaels**' "Murderers," **Carol Blys**' "Tale of Heroes," or **Ron Hansen**'s "Wickedness" gets me juiced in a way no novel can. The weaknesses of the collection: Where are the alternative voices like **John Barth**, **Robert Coover**, or **Jerry Bumpus**?

Vladimir Nabokov, *Ada or Ardor*. I read this to fill a remaining gap in my Nabokov list. The book does nothing to undermine Nabokov's reputation as prose master and brainiac, but it is very odd.

We're in an alternate universe, on the planet Demonia, which is our planet, but not. National borders have been scrambled. Much of our western Canada is a Russian-speaking province. Tartars rule Asia. The novel opens with the famous quotation from *Anna Karenina*, except in this world, it is unhappy families that are all alike. Two cousins provide the "ardor" of the title. But things aren't as they seem.

I'm glad I read *Ada*, and glad to have it behind me. Reading Nabokov, I always know that I am not smart enough, that I am unworthy. But in works like *Pale Fire*, he is a tolerant, even benevolent, big brother who allows me to tag along and feel pretty good about hanging out with the big guy. *Ada* left me feeling bludgeoned by Nabokov's display of brilliance. Yes, I'm not smart enough. Yes, I am unworthy. No más. No más.

After finishing *Ada*, I reread *Pnin*. All was well.

But wait! There's more: *Candide, The Confessions of St. Augustine, The Good Soldier,* seven or so volumes by

Ambrose Bierce, some **Kipling**, most of **Shaw**'s plays, several volumes of **Twain**, **Burton**'s translation of *The Book of the Thousand Nights and a Night* (all 16 volumes), **Sean Carroll's** *From Eternity to Here*, a couple of **Baum**'s Oz stories, *The Federalist Papers,* some Chandler, including *The Long Goodbye,* and *The Simple Art of Murder*. To keep Chandler company, **Hammett**'s *Red Harvest.* And **Dickens**—pretty much all of Dickens. Plays by **Euripides** and **Aristophanes**, **Aeschylus** and **Sophocles**. History according to **David Kennedy** as well as **Thucydides**, **Plutarch**, **Dio**, and **Herodotus**. Some **Hawthorne**, and **Conan Doyle**, and **Conrad**—with the secret agent Verloc rubbing shoulders with **le Carre**'s *A Perfect Spy*. And on and on.

Well, yes, I have an eBook reader. Everything in the last paragraph is just bits and bytes—some purchased, some out-of-copyright and downloaded free. These aren't so much to be read anytime soon. They are a crutch that makes it easier for me to pull their physical counterparts from my shelves and still enjoy the biblio-acquisitiveness of the personal library builder. And if late at night I just have to reread "The Lagoon," there it is along with the rest of **Conrad**.

VALERIE BROOKS

Valerie Brooks is a novelist, arts activist, Francophile and autodidact. During her 20s, she explored life as a visual artist, in her 30s she survived as an arts and education marketing specialist, and by age 40, she found her passion in fiction.

The genre has led her to fellowships, an associate editorship at *Northwest Review*, and publication of her short story "Dead Children" in *Scent of Cedars: Thirty-two Promising Writers from the Pacific Northwest.* A short memoir, *Liberté*, gained rave reviews in the *Boston Globe* and can be found in *France: a Love Story. Women Write About the French Experience*.

Soon to go to her agent, Val's novel tells the story of how a secret pact between sisters threatens to destroy their lives. From the cultural confines of New Hampshire to betrayals in Oregon, their twisted history catches up with them, hurts others who love them, and sends them to Paris as adversaries.

When people say to her, "I'll see you in the funny papers," they're not kidding–she's "Val," the main character in the internationally syndicated cartoon "Stone Soup" by her best pal Jan Eliot. Valerie lives on the McKenzie River with her husband Daniel Connors. Her confessions about writing can be found on her blog Gobsmacked Writer.

http://gobsmackedwriter.blogspot.com/

I'm an eclectic reader. I'll read almost anything about Paris. I love memoir and literary fiction. I listen to mysteries, thrillers, noir, plus young adult novels in my car on my long road trips back and forth to town and to the coast for writers' retreats. Areas of interest include the arts, feminism, politics, psychology, war, suicide, cultural movements, music, and childhood conditioning. What I read is usually connected to what I'm writing at the time. Right now, I'm interested in stories about sisters, moms and daughters, and how our early childhood environment forms us. I'm especially drawn to stories about powerful women. On my bed stand (some on my Kindle), recently read:

Cheryl Strayed, *Wild: From Lost to Found on the Pacific Crest Trail*. If you haven't heard about Cheryl's memoir, I can only imagine you're living as a hermit and should slip into your nearest bookstore to buy this emotionally honest and unflinching tale of coming to terms with the loss of a beloved mother. (Read my blog entry "Being Cheryl Strayed" for why this memoir means so much to me.)

Heidi Julavits, *The Vanishers, a Novel.* I dare you to put this down. At the other end of the spectrum from Cheryl's memoir, this novel, described as "a wildly imaginative and emotionally intense novel about mothers, daughters, and the psychic damage women can inflict on one another," is so much more than that. Just the voice alone will drag you into this suspenseful, crazy, astral-tripping story.

Deborah Lawrenson, *The Lantern.* An atmospheric, sensual, lyrical and modern gothic novel. Inspired by **Daphne du Maurier**'s *Rebecca*, the story moves slowly and hypnotically through the Provence lavender fields and the unraveling of a relationship.

Karen Moller, *Technicolor Dreamin': The 1960's Rainbow and Beyond.* One of my favorite memoirs, and not just because I love the 60s, bohemians, and fashion. Artist and fashion consultant Moller gives us a feminist perspective on her adventures in Beatnik San Francisco and New York, hip Paris, and swinging London. She knows many of the famous artists and writers of those times, but I was most happy to see her include Jim Haynes, ex-pat now living in Paris, who influenced so many during the Fluxus movement. Don't let the book's title and cover lead you to believe this is just a romp through the psychedelic 60s. This memoir is, above all, a critical observation of the counterculture.

Leymah Gbowee with **Carol Mithers**, *Mighty Be Our Powers: How Sisterhood, Prayer and Sex Changed a Nation at War.* When I first read this title, I immediately thought of *Lysistrata*, **Aristophanes**' Greek play from 411 B.C.E. about how women turned the tide of war by withholding sex. I still get chills whenever I think of young Gbowee turning loss, grief, and terror into the Liberian Mass Action for Peace, a coalition of Christian and Muslim women who sat in public protest, confronting Liberia's ruthless president and rebel warlords. Can we even imagine the courage that took? When you're feeling powerless, read this memoir.

Jay Asher, *Thirteen Reasons Why*. A YA thriller I read with my granddaughter. Small actions have large repercussions in this story about a teen suicide and how tapes left behind tell what led to her action. Highly recommended for parents with teens who will read the book together and discuss afterward.

Jo Nesbo & Don Bartlett, *The Leopard*. After listening to *The Girl with the Dragon Tattoo* in my car, followed by the next two novels in the trilogy, I was still hungering for more Scandinavian noir to fill those hours on the road. What I loved about those books were the atmospheric chill and entry to a new landscape that included politics, gender, relationships, family, revenge and, yes, psychopaths. Before *The Leopard*, I listened to Nesbo's *The Snowman* and found it compelling, but his follow up novels, including this one, seemed to be the same novel but with more gore and not enough depth.

Chris Pavone, *The Expats*. Some of the early reviews caught my interest in this "expats and espionage" novel set in Luxembourg. I remembered how much I love smart, literate espionage stories such as **le Carre**'s *Tinker, Tailor, Soldier, Spy,* but sorry to say this one wasn't that well told. The main character, Kate, is rarely in scene as she tells her story, and the so-called twists don't overcome the repetition, mediocre writing, and cardboard characters.

DICK CUMMINS

Dick is a venerable (hoary in fact) graduate of the Iowa Writers' Workshop, who left the "disappointment business" of writing in 1979 when his agent dumped him—the cruelest rejection and hard to ignore he points out. To get revenge he started an educational software company specializing in writing software for Apple II home computers—called it *Writing Software International*—hoping to grow into the name. His little company attracted venture capital and with munificent compensation of other people's money, Dick learned to fly and bought a used airplane. Several months later he promptly dead-sticked it into a Midwestern cornfield when the engine blew up—an exciting story for another time he says. At 70, Dick is just getting back into writing. And with a vengeance say the editors!

Books by my bed, under it, scattered around, in and on the dog bed—why we leave it there I don't know, as retriever Sunny and part Akita Sassy Anne jump up on our queen as if it were going to be a two-dog night every night, except in the summer here in San Diego when lows are stable around 68 degrees. Anyway, in no particular order but just as I noted them after walking in there:

Maxwell Perkins and John Hall Wheelock, *Editor to Author: The Letters of Maxwell E. Perkins*. Okay, but not what I was hoping for. Not done; may not finish. Have fallen asleep two nights in a row trying to get into it.

Beryl Markham, *West With the Night*. Really written by **Raoul Schumacher**, her third husband and a ghostwriter in Hollywood. Hemingway said of Markham, she "can write rings around all of us who consider ourselves writers . . ." and he was right, about Schumacher anyway. I have 600 hours in my pilot's log book and of course love this book—not just because of the exciting tales of early aviation in Africa but because of the elegant and exciting writing too! Highly recommended. (Have actually read many trenchant passages several times!)

Roy Blount, Jr., *Roy Blount's Book of Southern Humor*. Some excellent and very funny stuff—various authors I had never heard of—but should have! And of course **William Price Fox** too.

Abraham Pais, *Subtle Is the Lord: The Science and the Life of Albert Einstein*. Had to skip most formulas. Beyond my ken, but best quotes: "The difference between politics and science is that politics looks for the perfect compromise—while science looks for perfect truth." And my fave: "Time is so everything doesn't happen at once." — Einstein

Dick's Second Post

Rebecca Skloot, *The Immortal Life of Henrietta Lacks*. Nonfiction history about the billion-dollar living-tissue culture industry. Henrietta was an African-American woman who died very painfully of cervical cancer at Johns Hopkins in 1950; her cells, taken without her knowledge, wouldn't die in a Petri dish after the biopsy, and they have been vital in research in the 60 years since—cultured and sold for research because unlike all other human cells up until then—they just would not die!

Neither she nor her family have ever gotten a dime from the use of them, even though (tiny as they are) her cells—if stretched end to end—would circle the earth. The book is filled with make-your-blood-boil stuff and lots of fascinating, in-depth tissue science too!

Blake Bailey, *A Tragic Honesty: The Life and Work of Richard Yates*. Every night a series of mini-depressions reading of yet another one of Dick's breakdowns—I had him for Forms of Fiction in the Workshop in '67, and a few classes of Fiction before a classroom psychotic episode led to another commitment.

Charles J. Shields, *And So It Goes: Kurt Vonnegut: A Life*.

A bio of Kurt Vonnegut. I have about half of a review written for this but bogged down when I got to some of the negative stuff in his life—felt like I would be hurting his feelings to write it up or something—even though he's dead now, so not possible. But still…

Anthony Bukoski, *Time Between Trains.* Excellent stories. I should do a rave review for Amazon! "The 100-year-old confessional from St. Adalbert's that needs stripping to remove the patina of a century of old sins!" The story of a gay Polish waiter with a PhD in Philosophy who talks an illiterate, straight construction worker into moving in with him to share expenses—tells lies to his girlfriends to run them off—a story with insight and understanding for straights, not understanding as from read-a-book, but how it "feels" to be and understand the narrator. Nice irony and writing lilts on every page!

Erica Heller, *Yossarian Slept Here: When Joseph Heller Was Dad, the Apthorp Was Home, and Life Was a Catch-22*. By Joe Heller's daughter. A tell-all that humanizes the author of one of the most influential satirical novels depicting the insanity of WWII. Just reread *Catch-22* and it wasn't as good as it seemed in 1966—Joe never met an adverb he didn't like, which was the style then and he put them all in every dialogue tag it seems. But some chapters will always be classics of the war satire genre.

Nelson Algren, *The Neon Wilderness*. Circa 1950. Found the paperback at a yard sale—50 cents—best four bits I ever spent! Gritty stuff and as Hemingway said of him, "To read Algren you need to be able to take a punch."

David Nichols, ed., with a foreword by **Studs Terkel**, *Ernie's War: The Best of Ernie Pyle's World War II Dispatches*. This book was in my mother's library and I found it going through storage. She read *Here is Your War* and *Brave Men* to me when

I was about five years old and explained all the big vocabulary as she went along. (In first grade, Mrs. Romans wanted to know how I learned to talk like an adult and my mother said "the blame rested entirely on Ernie Pyle".)

If you want to read something that will water your chin, try this: http://www.unifiedpatriots.com/2011/05/28/the-death-of-captain-waskow-by-ernie-pyle. I think it was Hemingway who said that it is not only how you write, but what you write about that moves the reader.

William Price Fox, *Dixiana Moon*; *Lunatic Wind: Surviving the Storm of the Century*; *Satchel Paige's America*; and *Wild Blue Yonder*. He was the only instructor that ever edited a piece of mine line by line, as he thought it might get picked up by a magazine editor friend he knew. And he got me an agent too, after I sent him a screenplay in the mid-'70s.

And as with Kurt Vonnegut's style, you can't neatly classify Bill's stuff either—not as just "Southern" writing or just "magazine" writing or just "humor for the everyman." One reviewer called him the "…new Mark Twain of the South," and I always remember the simple advice he gave us about writing: "The only crime you can commit as a writer is to be boring."

In the preface to *Lunatic Wind*, Bill says he recorded "about 43 thousand feet of tape" interviewing people who had lived through Hurricane Hugo in 1989. Then he wrote up their experiences using "fictional techniques." Believe me, it was like you were right there, up to your neck in the lashing wind and rising waters and you had no idea if you were going to make it or not!

Peter Desberg and **Jeffrey Davis,** *Show Me the Funny!: At the Writers' Table with Hollywood's Top Comedy Writers*. With chapters like "My Mother the Sociopath" and "Write Yiddish, Cast British!" how can you go wrong? Also seems like all TV comedy writing is done by committee at the morning "writers' table," where frequent fistfights break out. The authors give well-known TV comedy writers a set piece plot and tell them to make it funny. I soon quit reading them because, well, it turned out to be the opposite of "showing me the funny."

James Salter, *The Hunters: A Novel*, and *Light Years*. Heard about this author from a friend. The first book was published in 1956 and is about the Korean War. The author was an F-86 fighter pilot and, as just a "single engine land" pilot, I loved all the flying stuff.

But it is the writing that wins the day. Some kudos: "There is scarcely a writer alive who could not learn from his passion and precision of language." — Peter Matthiessen. And: "...curl up for a flight with *The Hunters* through 'skies so clear you can see tomorrow.'" — *The New York Times Book Review* (1957). Haven't started *Light Years*, but looking forward to it—and to anything else Salter has written!

Jonah Lehrer, *Imagine: How Creativity Works*. A book about the creative process, areas of the brain that handle writing, art, working improv without a net, stand-up, also ad writing and at the end, a discussion of Shakespeare's London (times of "genius clusters") and how the Puritans not only closed down the theaters of London, but also the minds of the Londoners, too. (Sound familiar? That's because the Puritans came over here.)

From a review: "It is with persuasive chutzpah that Lehrer describes right-hemisphere operations in Bob Dylan's brain releasing him from the constrictions of early fame to recombine multiple musical influences into a revolutionary new song. Lehrer talks to a brain researcher who explains that the right hemisphere helps you see the forest, while the left is better for identifying the trees. The left handles denotation and clarifies while the right deals with *connotation*." (Nice.) Chapters: "*The Unconcealing*," "*The Letting Go*," "*The Outsider*," and "*The Shakespeare Paradox*."

I highly recommend it, and it hit number-one on the *NYT* bestseller list of nonfiction titles soon after its release. Guess a lot of people want to understand creativity!

Note: Not long after I read the book, the author really stepped on his literary schtick. Turns out he'd made up the Dylan quotes and Houghton Mifflin withdrew the book from publication (though it still is apparently available from Cannongate Books, a British publisher). See the account of this fiasco in the August 1, 2012 *Boston Globe*: http://www.bostonglobe.com/lifestyle/style/2012/08/01/jonah-lehrer-book-pulled-boston-based-publisher-houghton-mifflin-harcourt-after-author-admits-fabrication/R64AXel66XZbh5lOJipV3K/story.html

DAVID DAVIS

David Davis is a journalist based in Los Angeles. He is a contributing writer at *Los Angeles Magazine* and a contributing editor at *SportsLetter* (published by the LA84 Foundation). He's also the author of two books, *Showdown at Shepherd's Bush: The 1908 Olympic Marathon and the Three Runners Who Started a Running Craze* and *Marathon Crasher: The Life and Times of Merry Lepper, The First American Woman to Run a Marathon.* He is currently working on his next book: a biography of Duke Kahanamoku, to be published by the University of Nebraska Press.

I've stopped buying new books.

Please don't hold that against me, fellow writers. My partner was just laid off from her job and, as you've probably heard, freelancing is sketchy these days. Fun times.

But I am lucky. Where I live, just north of downtown Los Angeles, I'm near three public libraries: L.A., Pasadena, and Glendale. I'm also a member of the L.A. County Library system, as well as the Beverly Hills Library.

My nightstand has become a personal circulation desk, and it only costs me gas money.

I keep the library cards in the glove compartment of the car and, while I'm doing errands, I'll swing by the stately main branches. I like to browse the "new arrivals" section. The randomness makes it a form of literary roulette: What swag will I stumble across today? Last time was **John Jeremiah Sullivan**'s *Pulphead: Essays*. It's a gem, a collection of reportage that reads like short stories. I was so impressed that I later checked out Sullivan's first book, a memoir entitled *Blood Horses: Notes of a Sportswriter's Son*.

At the library, I find I'm more open to the possibility. I've picked up books about birth order and about California native plants because they looked, well, interesting. When I heard **Karl Marlantes** speak on the radio about his memoir, *What It Is Like to Go to War*, I jotted down the title. His searing account of serving in Vietnam was a memorable, sobering read. Another time, when I was interviewing a woman for a story about youth sports, she casually mentioned a book called *Cholos & Surfers*, by **Jack Lopez**, that I had not heard of. I tracked it down at a local branch and was glad that I did. It offers a perspective on the SoCal surfing scene that I'd never encountered before.

I've been on a biography tear of late in preparation for what I hope will be my next book. So, I read *George F. Kennan: An American Life*, by **John Lewis Gaddis**, and *Evel: The High-Flying Life of Evel Knievel: American Showman, Daredevil, and Legend* by **Leigh Montville**. Talk about opposites: Kennan, the preeminent diplomat-scholar during the Cold War, was the "father of containment." Knievel's mission was, simply, to soar.

There's one other advantage to library books. If at any point I'm bored or confused or overwhelmed—maybe it's the prose, maybe it's the subject matter—I'll stop reading. Case in point: **Arnold Schwarzenegger**'s memoir, *Total Recall: My Unbelievably True Life Story*, written with **Peter Petre**. The rags-to-riches part of his life was fascinating; the movie-star-to-governor section was as bloated as one of his films. I put it down and felt no guilt.

Another book awaits on the nightstand, wrapped tightly in a plastic cover, due back sometime next week.

KARIN EVANS

Karin Evans is the author of *The Lost Daughters of China: Adopted Girls, Their Journey to America, and the Search for a Missing Past*; *The Grace to Race: The Wisdom and Inspiration of the 80-Year-Old World Champion Triathlete known as The Iron Nun*; and the forthcoming *We're All Walking Home in the Dark*.

The Lost Daughters chronicles the experience of the author as she and her husband adopt two little girls from China, and it explores the backdrop of events that led to the international adoption of more than 100,000 orphaned girls from that country.

The Grace to Race is about Sister Madonna Buder, now 82, who recently completed the Canadian Ironman, becoming the first 82-year-old ever to do so. Then she went on to the Kona, Hawaii, Ironman as well. That Ironman event involves a 2.4-mile swim, 112 miles of cycling, and a full 26-mile marathon. Whew.

We're All Walking Home in the Dark is historical fiction, based on the intermingled lives of a Tang Dynasty female poet in China and a 21st-century burned-out journalist in San Francisco.

Karin's also working on a chapbook of poetry, *Not Quite Home*. And she's a certified Yoga instructor.

I always have a stack teetering beside my bed, dipping into it depending on mood and what's reachable. Just now I'm most deeply into *The Other Wes Moore: One Name, Two Fates* by **Wes Moore**. This stunning bit of nonfiction, which chronicles the lives of two boys growing up in Baltimore, whose lives take different directions (one a Rhodes Scholar, the other convicted of murder and sentenced to life), has been required reading for some incoming college classes this year. I'm deeply touched by both of these lives and the book resonates just as loudly in Berkeley as it does in Baltimore.

I'm alternating that with the delightful new book, *The Swan*, a fresh-voiced novel by my friend **Jim Cohee**. Billed as a "fictional memoir," it is told in the charmingly eccentric voice of a highly imaginative ten-year-old who is coping with a family tragedy as best he can by slipping into fantasy. It's a spare, haunting, and beautifully told story.

Some nights I pick up the heaviest book in the pile: *Where on Earth is Heaven?* by BBC producer and filmmaker **Jonathan Stedall**. Stedall ponders all the big questions, through explorations of the thoughts of **Tolstoy**, **Rudolph Steiner**, **Teilhard de Chardin**, and anyone else he encountered who has also probed the meaning of life.

As I dipped through the pile to see what else is lying in wait for my evening hours, I unearthed one book that could have made a difference, and still might, if I can keep it from getting reburied: **Karen Kingston**'s *Clear Your Clutter with Feng Shui*.

JENNIE FIELDS

Jennie Fields was born in Chicago and raised in Highland Park, Illinois. She received her BFA in creative writing from the University of Illinois, and an MFA in fiction in 1976 from the Iowa Writers' Workshop, which helped to toughen her up for her next career: advertising. After 32 years of writing McDonald's jingles and dreaming up green moths to help sell sleeping pills (all the while writing novels), she left New York to live with her husband in Nashville, Tennessee, and write fiction full-time. Her fourth book, *The Age of Desire*—a biographical novel based on Edith Wharton's late-life love affair with a young journalist—was published by Viking in 2012 and is now also available as a Penguin Paperback. She has a 27-year-old daughter and two grown stepchildren. She and her personal trainer... er...dog, Violet Jane, walk five miles every day searching for answers to all literary questions.

http://jenniefields.com/

At the moment, the books by my bed include:

Wintering: A Novel of Sylvia Plath by **Kate Moses** and *A Good Hard Look* by **Ann Napolitano**. I was on a panel with both at the Key West Literary Seminar and am looking forward to enjoying their writing. I also have:

Richard Russo, *That Old Cape Magic*. Still on the pile. About a professor, Jack Griffin, driving around Cape Cod with the ashes of his deceased parents in the trunk of his car. From a review in *Publisher's Weekly*: "Crafting a dense, flashback-filled narrative that stutters across two summer outings to New England (and as many weddings), Russo (*Empire Falls*) convincingly depicts a life coming apart at the seams, but the effort falls short of the literary magic that earned him a Pulitzer."

Sue Miller, *The Good Mother*. I have read it again after many years. I still think it a watershed book—one of the best books about women written in the last 30 years.

Ian McEwan, *Amsterdam* and *Saturday*. Oh how I loved

Saturday. What tour de force: the entire book takes place in a single day! *Amsterdam* is dark and funny. It almost feels written by a different author. Worth reading, though.

Joyce Carol Oates, *The Falls*. This is my favorite Oates book so far, not that I've read every single one—but maybe ten. Who could read them all? She's the most prolific writer in the universe!

Marilynne Robinson, *Gilead*, and *Home*. Robinson is extraordinary, poetic, one of a kind.

And all of **Edith Wharton**—which isn't exactly by the bed. Edith has her own *two* shelves in my bookcase. I read her again and again. I am also reading *The Buccaneers*. Sadly, she died before finishing it, and someone else (Marion Mainwaring) attempted an ending—probably not a good idea!

I also go back to **Stegner**, **Carol Shields**, **Anne Tyler**, and **Colm Toibin**, and *Revolutionary Road* by **Richard Yates**.

In the queue are:

T.C. Boyle, *World's End* and *When the Killing's Done*. I tried to read *World's End* and couldn't, hence it's no longer in the queue. Too Quixotic for me. Instead, I'm almost done with *When the Killing's Done*. Terrific. Boyle's often SO good, it floors me!

Ethan Canin, *America America*. He's a great short story writer. I don't know what to expect of this.

Ian McEwan, *In Between the Sheets* and *The Comfort of Strangers*.

Scott Spencer, *Man in the Woods*. I love Scott Spencer's

Endless Love, one of the greatest books ever written, and a book completely destroyed by the bad movie version.

Marina Fiorato, *The Glassblower of Murano*. I just had a lovely trip to Venice. Maybe this will bring it back to me. I'm not even sure where I picked this up.

Billy Collins, *Ballistics: Poems*. Billy was also at the Key West Literary Seminar. He's the most entertaining poet I've ever seen. At the same time, he's quite subtle, quite brilliant.

Oh, and I just ordered another Iowa classmate, **Mike Harris**' new book, *The Chieu Hoi Saloon*. Looking forward to it. Mike was so kind to come to a reading of mine in San Diego, miles from his home in L.A., and I've yet to read his book. I am a bad person.

HARVEY FREEDENBERG

Harvey Freedenberg practices intellectual property law and litigation with a Harrisburg, Pennsylvania law firm. In 2000, he took a six-month sabbatical from his law practice and studied creative writing with novelist Susan Perabo at his alma mater, Dickinson College. Four of his short stories have won prizes, and he has written an as yet unpublished novel. Harvey, a member of the National Book Critics Circle, reviews both fiction and nonfiction for BookPage, Bookreporter.com, Shelf Awareness and the *Minneapolis Star Tribune* and writes a monthly column on books for *Harrisburg Magazine*. He can be found on Twitter at @HarvF and Facebook: https://www.facebook.com/harvey.freedenberg

I'm in the happy situation of living in a house where the

nearest book is never more than a few feet away, but our overstuffed bookshelves bear witness to the difficulty of finding room for all of them. Though a Kindle has helped stem the tide, it's inevitable that small islands have surfaced next to more than one bed.

Since I began reviewing in 2005, my bedside table has become the resting place for an ever-shifting array of titles that remind me of the deadline-driven reading that lies ahead in the next few weeks. Right now that space is occupied by: *Canada,* the new novel from one of my favorite writers, Pulitzer Prize winner **Richard Ford**; liberal commentator **E.J. Dionne's** *Our Divided Political Heart*, an election-year analysis of our pervasive political gridlock; *What Happened to Sophie Wilder*, **Christopher Beha**'s novel about belief and doubt; and new essay collections from two very smart people—**Marilynne Robinson**'s *When I Was a Child I Read Books* and **Jonathan Franzen**'s *Farther Away: Essays.*

The pull of that professional reading means that worthy volumes of short stories by **Deborah Eisenberg** (*Twilight of the Superheroes: Stories)*, **Max Apple** (*The Jew of Home Depot and Other Stories),* and **George Saunders** (*In Persuasion Nation)* I once placed there with the best of intentions have been relegated to a second stack, along with **T.S. Eliot**'s *Four Quartets* and the slim book, *Slow Reading,* by **John Miedema**, which seems like a rebuke to the whole notion of a TBR pile. Short stories and poems remain there because somehow they seem less intimidating, more approachable, than a fat, untouched novel would in that space, but I don't delude myself that I'll get to them anytime soon

The more interesting collection is the one I've assembled in what used to be my daughter's bedroom, converted to a branch library/guestroom a few years after she left for college. I've gathered this group of books with some care and like to picture it as a pile of stones marking a path through the woods or a signal fire in the desert. The books that have made it there are ideal to pick up for a few minutes of pleasurable reading before dropping off to sleep or for companionship in the middle of a restless night:

J. Peder Zane's *The Top Ten: Writers Pick Their Favorite Books* is a compilation of the favorite books of more than 100 authors, while **Leah Price**'s *Unpacking My Library: Writers and Their Books* is a mini coffee-table book boasting gorgeous color photographs highlighting the libraries of writers like **Jonathan Lethem**, **Gary Shteyngart**, and others. *A Book of Luminous Things: An International Anthology of Poetry*, edited by **Czeslaw Milosz**, rests atop a pile that includes essay collections by **Donald Hall** (*Eagle Pond)*; **Joseph Epstein** (*Narcissus Leaves the Pool* and *In a Cardboard Belt)*; **Ian Frazier** (*Lamentations of the Father)*; and the ultimate bibliophile, **Nicholas Basbanes** (*Editions & Impressions: My Twenty Years on the Book Beat)*, alongside the timeless *Meditations* of **Marcus Aurelius**. All are rich with wisdom, inspiration, humor and consolation, some of the rewards we seek when we reach for a good book. What more could one ask from a dozen or so volumes? It's enough to make me want to tiptoe over there for some late night reading and my only wish is that our guests appreciate them as much as I do.

CATHERINE GAMMON

Catherine Gammon was born in Los Angeles, California. She earned a BA in philosophy at Pomona College, and an MFA in fiction from the Iowa Writers' Workshop in 1976.

Catherine was a fellow of the Fine Arts Work Center in Provincetown in 1977 and 1981, and worked for many years in the type production department of the *New York Review of Books*. In 1991 her novel *Isabel Out of the Rain* was published by Mercury House, and in 1992 she joined the faculty of the MFA program at the University of Pittsburgh.

Her fiction has appeared in *Ploughshares, The North American Review, Kenyon Review, Manoa, Central Park, Fiction International, Other Voices,* and other journals. She served as fiction editor for *Cape Discovery*, an anthology of fiction and poetry by Fine Arts Work Center fellows. Her latest novel, *Sorrow*, was just released by Braddock Avenue Books.

https://www.facebook.com/catherine.gammon.sorrow

Catherine has received NEA and New York Fellowship for the Arts grants for her fiction, as well as a creative research fellowship from the American Antiquarian Society for work in the Esther Forbes Papers and the Cotton Mather collection in preparation for a novel about the Salem witchcraft trials.

In 2001 she left both the academy and the literary marketplace to begin residential training at San Francisco Zen Center. In 2005 she was ordained a Soto Zen priest by Tenshin Reb Anderson, and in 2010 served as Shuso, or head monk, for the spring practice period at Green Dragon Temple/Green Gulch Farm.

In January 2011 she returned to Pitt's MFA program as a visiting professor, and hopes to continue reweaving her life in writing into her life in Zen.

http://catherinegammon.wordpress.com/

When Eric Olsen came to interview me for *We Wanted To Be Writers*, I didn't give him any titles for "Books by the Bed." My reading at that time was entirely devoted to dharma study, and I didn't think those books, wonderful as they are, were quite what this feature was meant to be about. But a few things I've been reading lately move me finally to step up and offer a few words.

Jaimy Gordon, *Lord of Misrule*. It's no longer by the bed because I loaned it to someone to read. I loved this book. It was so satisfying to read a novel so well written, so warm, so intimate with and respectful of its characters, so wise, so mature, so full of life and darkness and heart. I had just before read *A Visit From the Goon Squad* by **Jennifer Egan**, which was a good read, timely and smart, even made me cry somewhere along the way, but on some level, it felt kind of like watching well done, intelligent television—and I can be an addict of well done television, don't get me wrong—but what was the literary appreciation about? I didn't get it, and I felt kind of helplessly, hopelessly out of the cultural loop, even over the hill. Perhaps I exaggerate. After all, my taste has always been a little, or a lot, out of synch. But then I picked up *Lord of Misrule.* I hesitate to use the word redemption, but there it is. A long shot that became a winner. And full of love.

Bill McKibben, *Eaarth: Making a Life on a Tough New Planet*. Irreversible climate change is already happening—does this surprise anyone? Bill McKibben's account, already a year out of date, makes the case so clearly, I recommend it as a must read. McKibben's perspective is global and his argument is that we already live on an altered planet, no longer the earth we're accustomed to (hence the gimmicky nod to renaming, Eaarth with two A's)—that no matter what we do now to respond we will not be able to do business or culture or politics as they have been done until now. But this possibly depressing news is only the first half of the book.

The second demonstrates with example after example the capacity of people joining together locally in work (and protest and play) to create resilient and sustainable ways of living that respond to the change. I found the book's tone occasionally a little glib and snarky, but only occasionally and only a little, not nearly so much as to undermine the informed, wise, and inspiring insight offered.

And relating this book to the ongoing conversation around writer as public figure, I can only point to McKibben as a writer who fully takes that responsibility on.

Derek Jarman, *Chroma: A Book of Color*. A tale from the fuddling, failing side of memory—collecting my stored boxes of books, left behind in Pittsburgh during my ten years in California, sorting, deciding what to keep and what to pass along, I come to *Chroma.* I remember it, but vaguely. I read around in it, I think, but not cover to cover. I will pass it on, but in particular—it is right for my daughter, a filmmaker, Heather von Rohr, or my friend the painter Deborah Morris. I email them together, would one of them like it? My daughter loved that book and has it in storage and says if Deborah doesn't want it she'll take it and give it to someone. Hmm. Heather, I write, could this copy be yours? No, she's sure it's stored. But maybe she gave it to me? Oh, yes. I think she's right. I'm not sure that this confusion can be appreciated if your own memory is not beginning to lose itself this way. But by now I'm deep in the colors, Jarman's haunting mix of memoir and meditations on color, a slim assemblage of brief quotations, contemplations, and personal stories, written as he was dying, profoundly simple, straightforward, and formally inspiring. One short little chapter each night. When I finish, it goes to Deborah.

Blake Butler, *There Is No Year*. Butler is new to me. I don't know how long he's been a star or how widely he is read, especially among my Workshop generation. I recently discovered him during a short stay in Provincetown, browsing the wealth of literary magazines in the fellows lounge at the Fine Arts Work Center. His words stood out from the pages, the rhythms and tones. Now this. This novel is a mystery. Old-fashioned, I wish it were printed on plain white paper, instead of on gray. The words are enough, and the gray is discouraging to aging eyes. Maybe the aging aren't meant to read this book. But try, old eyes and all. I haven't finished, have yet to see where the journey is going. But it goes, and there is magic in it, compelling and strange.

JOE HALDEMAN

Joe Haldeman was born in Oklahoma City. He grew up in Puerto Rico, New Orleans, Washington, DC, and Alaska. Drafted in 1967, he fought in the Central Highlands of Vietnam as a combat engineer and received the Purple Heart. His first book, *War Year*, is based on his experience in the war.

He earned a BS in Physics and Astronomy at the University of Maryland, followed by graduate work in math and computer science, but he dropped out to write, eventually completing his MFA in fiction at the University of Iowa Writers' Workshop in 1975.

Joe lives in Gainesville, Florida and Cambridge, Massachusetts with his wife of forty-four years, Gay. He has been a part-time professor at the Massachusetts Institute of Technology since 1983, and has taught writing workshops at Michigan State (Clarion), Clarion West Seattle, SUNY Buffalo, Princeton, University of North Dakota, Kent State, and the University of North Florida. He has also worked as a statistician's assistant (HEW), librarian, computer programmer, musician, laborer, occasional platform speaker, and consultant.

Since *War Year*, Joe has published more than 30 books, including *The Forever War* (1974), perhaps his best-known novel. Among his most recent books are *Work Done for Hire*, *Earthbound*, *Starbound*, *Marsbound,* and *The Accidental Time Machine*.

Some titles have been published in as many as 20 languages. Dozens of Joe's short stories, novelettes, and novellas have appeared in various science fiction magazines, along with a few appearances in "mainstream" magazines such as *Playboy*. He has also published songs and poetry, primarily in smaller magazines, but also in *Harper's* and *Omni*.

Several of his books have been made into movies or

adapted for the stage. Joe has been awarded his genre's highest honors multiple times, including the Hugo, Nebula, Ditmar, Rhysling, World Fantasy, and John W. Campbell awards. In 2012 he was inducted into the Science Fiction Hall of Fame.

http://www.joehaldeman.com/books

When I go to bed I fall asleep immediately. The little stack of books I have there goes back a couple of years to when I had a cold and was stuck in bed—*The Portable Faulkner*; *The Portable James Joyce*; *Love Among the Haystacks and Other Stories*, **D.H. Lawrence**; *The Collector*, **John Fowles**; and *The Turn of the Screw and Other Short Novels,* **Henry James**. Pretty classy stuff. But it's been years since I opened one.

More recently, I've been going through an Emily Dickinson phase, reading *Dickinson: Selected Poems and Commentaries* by **Helen Vendler**, and *A Summer of Hummingbirds* by **Chistopher Benfey**. Vendler's collection/ exegesis of Dickinson is diverting, but not as interesting as the one she did about Shakespeare's sonnets.

Both poets are mysterious figures, but of course Shakespeare trumps everyone in that regard. I really liked *A Summer of Hummingbirds*, about the "intricate map of friendship, family, and romance" among Dickinson, Mark Twain, Harriet Beecher Stowe, and Martin Johnson Heade in the summer of 1881. What a magical time! (I bought it at the Dickinson House in Amherst.) Writers and artists who live in a community with others, of whatever ilk, can build something really special, if often fragile. I've had it a few times. Maybe while it's happening we don't value it enough. If you have any interest in the period or people, I'd highly recommend it.

DENISE HAMILTON

Former *Los Angeles Times* staff writer Denise Hamilton's crime novels have been finalists for the Edgar, Anthony, Macavity, and Willa Cather awards. Her new novel, *Damage Control*, received starred reviews from *Publishers Weekly* and *Library Journal*, raves from *USA Today*, *Los Angeles Magazine* and BN.com and kudos from James Ellroy ("A superb psychological thriller"). Denise's first series book and Edgar award finalist *The Jasmine Trade* is on sale as an e-book.

http://www.denisehamilton.com

Here are the books by my bed:

John Connolly, *The Infernals: A Samuel Johnson Tale*. I have two teenagers, so I read a lot of young-adult fiction to see what's out there that might interest my boys and also because I like the genre myself. So atop the YA pile is this sequel to Connolly's hilarious Halloween YA book *The Gates*, which came out two years ago. Connolly also writes very dark macabre thrillers for adults.

Chris Adrian, *The Great Night*. I've read excerpts of this novel in the *New Yorker* and love how Adrian reworks Shakespeare's *A Midsummer Night's Dream* in contemporary San Francisco. Enchanting!

Kiran Desai, *Hullabaloo in the Guava Orchard*. I love most of the Indian writers I've read, and some people told me that *Hullabaloo* has some gorgeous descriptions of food and scent. As the perfume columnist for the *Los Angeles Times Magazine*, I love to find books with fragrant angles.

Francesca Lia Block, *Pink Smog*. I have an ARC (advance review copy) of this because I'm reviewing it for the *Los*

Angeles Review of Books. I adore Francesca's writing. Urban contemporary fairy tales are one of my secret little passions.

What will never be beside my bed:

Ann Rule, *The Stranger Beside Me*. Years ago, true-crime queen Ann Rule worked a late night crisis hotline with a handsome, charming, self-deprecating young man she knew only as Ted. Rule, a Washington policewoman, was absolutely gobsmacked to learn later that the charming young man was notorious serial killer Ted Bundy and they'd sat together alone at 3 A.M., chatting and fielding calls. Her disbelief at being conned by Bundy and her natural curiosity led her to write one of the most chilling serial killer profiles I've ever read, a meditation on the heart of evil, how monsters like this can walk among us, unnoticed, and the need for caution. Because if savvy cop and true crime writer Ann Rule was taken in by Bundy, what chance do we have? I read this book in my living room at night while my family slept, the dog and cats around me, but I had to put it down and go upstairs and snuggle up to my sleeping husband to shake the dread and fear that enveloped me while reading this book.

ROSS HOWELL

Ross followed a career in academic fund-raising, public relations, book publishing, and marketing after receiving his MFA from the Iowa Writers' Workshop. He's now freelance editing and teaching part-time at Elon University. Recent stories have appeared in *The Sewanee Review* and *The Gettysburg Review*. He lives in Greensboro, NC, with his wife, Mary Leigh, English cocker spaniel diva, Pinot, and pit bull-Lab mix, Sam.

There's a great big novel on my night stand. And it's embarrassing. I'm probably the lone Writers' Workshop grad of Southern extraction who's reading **Allan Gurganus**'s *Oldest Living Confederate Widow Tells All* for the very first time.

If Allan sees this I don't know if he'll drive over from Hillsborough to whip my ass for waiting 30 years to buy his book or bring a preacher to ask the Lord's healing of my afflicted mind.

I picked up Allan's book for selfish reasons. I was working on an historical novel using third-person narration. Everything sounded stilted and contrived.

I hoped *Confederate Widow* might help. It did. With the first sentence it showed me I needed a first-person voice to carry the reader back in time. If there is a better example of such a voice than *Confederate Widow,* I haven't found it.

Other books? I always seem to learn from **D. H. Lawrence**. So there's *Sons and Lovers.* I'm reading it not only for its beauty but also because my father was a drunk. The scene where the mother sees in the moonlight she's covered with lily pollen after her drunken husband has locked her out of the house—I'd give anything to have written such a scene before my mother passed.

There's also *Collected Stories: D. H. Lawrence.* I grew up among the characters in "The Horse Dealer's Daughter." Same people—just different accents and continents and times. For some reason I'm able to learn more about writing about my region from someone like Lawrence, who comes at me over a span of distance and time and culture.

Still, I admire the writing of another workshop graduate, **John Yount**. John knows country people inside and out. Everybody should read *The Trapper's Last Shot*. The opening scene of the book is unforgettable—as powerful an existential statement as I have ever read. I met him by the good graces of a Workshop classmate, who'd studied with him at the University of New Hampshire.

And at the recommendation of my friend Gordon Mennenga, I have a stack of books by **William Gay**. Gay, a Tennessean, started writing at the age of 15 but had nothing published until his late 50s, when his career took off. Knowing my situation—I hadn't published fiction since 1985—Gordy thought Gay's success might encourage me. As always, Gordy, thanks. Gay's collection of stories, *I Hate to See That Evening Sun Go Down: Collected Stories*, is worth a read by anybody.

Also by the bed is **D. H. Lawrence's** *Studies in Classic American Literature*. The writing is mannered and odd, but I can't think of another work that so quickly arrives at the essence of great American authors like **Hawthorne**, **Whitman**, **Melville**, and others.

There's **Thomas Hardy's** *Jude the Obscure*. I always have a Hardy story, poem, or novel around. For the descriptions of the natural world.

Since I opened with an embarrassing admission, I'll close with one: The latest issue of *Vanity Fair* is always on my nightstand. I read the magazine cover to cover. I read Graydon Carter's editorial introduction. I read the photo captions naming elegant people at lavish cocktail parties, though I rarely recognize them. I read the little sidebars where the type is so small it practically requires a magnifying glass to see.

And can that **Christopher Hitchens** write or what? I read his article on the King James Bible, "When the King Saved God," over and over and over. The pages of the magazine are not quite the same, now that he's gone.

Books Not by Ross's Bed

Certain books cannot be allowed by my bed for the same reason it's not a good idea to let Lindsay Lohan have a cocktail or Anthony Weiner log on to his Twitter account.

William Faulkner's regal prose still mesmerizes me the way it did when I was an undergraduate at the University of Virginia, not that long after "Pappy" roamed the grounds of Mr. Jefferson's University, pronouncing the fraternity St. Anthony's Hall "the last bastion of Southern decadence" and teaching the odd writing class or two in his demure and inscrutable way.

The fact that I tried to make every undergrad piece I wrote sound like Faulkner didn't seem at the time to be a problem at all. The only fault I found in my prose style was that I couldn't seem to out-Faulkner Faulkner.

I mean, c'mon, **William Styron** had written *Lie Down in Darkness*, right? Who says you can't drink the whiskey and wake up from the hangover with your own recognizable style?

Fast-forward nearly forty years. Recently I had some pieces accepted. When I go back and read them, they sound the way I want them to sound. I feel pleased and comfortable.

At last, I've discovered my narrative style. God knows, it took long enough.

Therefore, at this time, these books by Faulkner are forbidden fruit on my nightstand:

Go Down, Moses. If I could only have one book while marooned on a desert island, it would be this one. I'm not sure how many times I've read the stories "Was" and "The Bear," but I'm sure I could read them countless times more, and still discover something new and brilliant in each reading.

Absalom, Absalom! Every novel I begin somehow evolves into a tale told by multiple narrators with conflicting points of view. That's a magnificent technique. Just look at **Jayne Anne Phillips**'s *Lark and Termite.* But I know I need to get one solid novel under my belt told from a single point of view—my concerto, if you will, before I try my symphony.

The Sound and the Fury. Well, there's the multiple-point-of-view thing, of course. But the big problem is the female character, Candace Compson. To me she's more seductive than Cleopatra, Emma Bovary, or Kate in *The Taming of the Shrew*.

I have to stay away from Caddy until some of my own female characters diminish her charms.

Maybe some day I'll be strong enough to read William Faulkner again, even my favorite stories and novels, and not allow his elegant rhythms to entwine themselves like wisteria into my own humble prose.

Just not yet.

TERRY JOHNSON

Terry D. Johnson is a lecturer of bioengineering at the University of California Berkeley. He is co-author of *How to Defeat Your Own Clone: And Other Tips for Surviving the Biotech Revolution.* He serves as a science advisor for film and television, and tweets, predictably, as @ terrydjohnson.

Books by my bed include:

Any Nero Wolfe novel. I'm with Wodehouse on this one—**Rex Stout** is endlessly re-readable, and that's a high standard to meet. The narrator gleefully discloses what it's like living and working with an eccentric genius, who is easy to respect and often very hard to like. I last re-read *Triple Jeopardy*, which is almost equal parts domestic farce and mystery.

James Gleick, *Genius: The Life and Science of Richard Feynman*. The best biography I've ever read! Richard Feynman worked on the Manhattan Project and the commission investigating the Challenger disaster. In between he won a Nobel prize. Throughout, he discovered a great deal of pleasure in life.

The latest **Terry Pratchett**. For me, *Unseen Academicals*, but only because I haven't gotten hold of *Snuff* yet. Pratchett's Discworld series began as a relatively straightforward parody of Howard and Tolkien, but quickly evolved into a place where he could tackle any issue he cared to from an earnest, absurdist angle. The best thing anyone ever said about my book was, "It read a bit Pratchetty."

VICTORIA M. JOHNSON

Victoria M. Johnson writes both fiction and nonfiction. *The Substitute Bride*, her short story collection out on Amazon and Smashwords, is Victoria's debut in the arena of indie publishing. Her other publications include *The Doctor's Dilemma*, a novel, and the nonfiction *Grant Writing 101*. Victoria is a blogger and film buff who writes and directs short films.

http://victoriamjohnson.com

First a little background. Books are my weakness. A house we had lived in for 19 years featured an enormous library with about two thousand books—and when we moved it was a substantial task to go through all the books and decide which to donate. I parted company with more than half. Our new house had large bookcases and it didn't take long to fill them up, in addition to bookcases in my office, and our bedroom bedside tables.

When we were forced to leave that lovely house due to foreclosure, it was a stressful time. We went from 1800 square feet to 800 square feet! Needless to say, I had difficulty culling through my book collection to make donations. But I did it, bringing only about 250 books with us. And I swore that I would only buy e-books from then on. I haven't exactly kept that promise, but I did keep the promise to have our bedroom clutter-free. No stacks of books and magazines and journals by the bed. Today I only have three items on my nightstand: a literary journal, a book of poetry, and a chapbook by a friend.

The chapbook is *Wild Place* by **Erica Goss**. I thought it would be a good idea to read a few pages to help me unwind and fall asleep. Wrong. Her poems struck a cord with me. One in particular poked and nudged me and kept me up most of the night until I finally went to my office to write a poem. I don't read this chapbook before bedtime anymore.

The journal is *Quarter After Eight*, Vol.18. It's a quirky journal with unpredictable pieces of short fiction, essays, memoirs, and poetry. This volume gets my creative juices flowing and urges me to run to my office to write. Also not a good choice for reading before bedtime.

The poetry is *The Curvature of Blue* by **Lucille Lang Day**. One of her other books, *Wild One*, is my all-time favorite book of poetry. And that was on my table before this one arrived in the mail. Lucille's poetry is many things: thought provoking, inspiring, intelligent, and deep. I always enjoy reading it.

Previously I would have stacks of nonfiction books, writer magazines, and blank journals to jot down my thoughts, as well as the single fiction book I was reading at the time, by the bedside. My fiction choices vary from romance to thrillers to short stories—those are all now kept in the office where they belong. I should also mention that we are planning another move, a really good one to Europe, and I have to pare down even more—no more than two boxes of books. Wish me luck!

GERI LIPSCHULTZ

Geri Lipschultz is a Jersey girl born in Newark and raised in Park Ridge, although she was long gone by the time Richard Nixon moved in with his condo placed on cleared land that had once been home to a meandering stream and forests. She graduated from UMass (Amherst) with a BA in Elementary Education, followed by an MFA in fiction from the Iowa Writers Workshop in 1976. She has published work in *The New York Times*, *College English*, *Kalliope*, *Black Warrior Review*, and other publications. A story of hers won the 2012 fiction award from *So to Speak: a Feminist Journal of Language and Art*. Her work is forthcoming in *Pearson's Introduction to Reading and Writing*, a College English anthology. She also has a story forthcoming in *Wreckage of Reason II: An Anthology of Contemporary Xxperimental Prose by Women Writers*.

She performed in her one-woman show, *Once Upon the Present Time*, produced in New York City by Woodie King, Jr. Her production, *Rising Above the Shadow—Women's Artistic Responses to September 11th*, featured the work of fifty women artists—painters, musicians, dancers, writers. Geri was awarded a CAPS grant from New York State for one of her novels. Her fiction was nominated for the Foley Award, and she was a Heekin semi-finalist.

A little more than thirty years after finishing her MFA, she decided to go back to school for the doctorate, which she finished in 2012. She now feels completely comfortable when her students call her "Professor." She lives in Huntington Station, New York, with her husband, Erwin Wong. Her two children, both aspiring violinists, are David (26), who mixes the classical with the electric, and Eliza (15), who at the moment, seems to prefer the classical tradition.

I've organized the following list of books by the bed into four groups: pre-PhD, PhD in process, pre-comps, and doctorate-in-hand.

Pre-Phd: Skyscrapers of books rising high under a table, against the wall, bunches of books, including: a (then) fairly new translation of **Dante**, *The Inferno*—**Robert** and **Jean**

Hollander's version; a biography of Oppenheimer by **Kai Bird** and **Martin J. Sherman**, *American Prometheus: The Triumph and Tragedy of J. Robert Oppenheimer*; a *Portable **Oscar Wilde***; **Jasper Fforde**'s *The Eyre Affair: a Thursday Next Novel,* a hilariously addictive romp in literary criminal shenanigans; **Philip Larkin**'s *Collected Poems*; **Jose Saramago**'s *Blindness;* an anthology opened up to a sonnet by **Donne**, "Batter my heart…"; and a book of **Frost**'s early poems, opened up to the poem about the woodpile—this mix reflecting both what to throw at my students and what will with any luck self-inspire.

PhD in process: Now to a land known for coal and poverty, Appalachian beauty, and its many writers, including my favorites: **Toni Morrison** and **James Wright** and **Sherwood Anderson**, whose "Death in the Woods," I will for the first time decide to use in my Creative Writing classes (from *Death in the Woods and Other Stories*). In Athens, Ohio—where the skyscrapers of books rose and fell, depending on the paper I was writing—the fallen books, those in my hands, next to my bed, included: **Tayeb Salih**'s *Season of Migration to the North*, a favorite, an arresting book, almost a cautionary tale, that I read for a class in postcolonial literature, about a Sudanese Don Juan, a brilliant scholar and lover, and a treachery within this man directed both at himself and those who had the misfortune to be attracted to him—many implications as to the source of this treachery; Nigerian novelist and poet, **Chris Abani**'s, *Song for Night*—powerful, disturbing narrative by a boy soldier; **Ngugi wa Thiong'o**'s *A Grain of Wheat;* and **Chinua Achebe**'s *Things Fall Apart.* Seminal books these all are, opening my eyes and my heart. Except for Achebe's, these were books I'm sure I would otherwise have never known. How much poorer I would have been!

Pre-comps: My penultimate entry here. Skyscrapers entirely toppled, a floor tiled with books; colored tabs jutting out from their pages; everywhere notes dotted with colored markers signaling a codified chaos. An expansive list I had with books ranging from **Rushdie** to **Coetzee**, from **Morrison** to **W.E.B. DuBois**, books of theory, novels, poetry, history. Postcolonial/ African American Literature, Literature of the Marginalized Voice—somewhere here was my intended expertise. At the moment of this post, I was knee-deep into a book titled *Oreo* by **Fran Ross**, an African American Jewish writer. Darkly funny, satiric, really, charting a girl's search for her Jewish father, a Joycean journey, with jokes that are sharp, almost-but-not offensive. Fran Ross wrote for Richard Pryor. I kept thinking I would ask my Black/Jewish nieces if they had known of the book; honestly, I never got around to it, but I did pass my comprehensive exams, and a year after that, I received the paper that is now framed in my little studio five hundred miles or so northeast of Athens, Ohio.

Doctorate-in-hand: Back to Long Island, preparing for Fall 2013 classes to teach in NYC, as an Adjunct Assistant Professor. Currently, closest to the pillow, are *A People's History of the United States* by **Howard Zinn** and two books by **Tim Weiner**, *Enemies: A History of the FBI* and *Legacy of Ashes: The History of the CIA*. Tim, a Pulitzer prize-winning journalist is someone I discovered only recently, having met his wife at Wellspring House, a lovely and unusual retreat for writers and artists.

The retreat itself is the brainstorm of a couple's plan for retirement. Preston Browning, an English professor, and his wife, architect Ann Hutt Browning (now deceased), decided fourteen years ago to relocate—to move from Chicago to western Massachusetts, where they would redesign an old carriage house and open up for business. It is the epitome of its name, located in Ashfield, an old New England hill town that has its own historical society, a small museum with assorted artifacts and photographs and documentation. Its library is named after the Belding silk manufacturing family, located not a thousand feet from Wellspring House, but there are enough books in the old, converted carriage house to keep anyone from plucking from her own collection and lugging them along. At Wellspring House, I had *A People's History* by my bed, and although I leafed through it, I couldn't settle in, and somehow preferred novels and stories.

Emily Bronte's *Wuthering Heights* and **Aldous Huxley**'s *Brave New World*, along with some of **Tolstoy**'s stories were among the books that I brought to my nightstand at Wellspring House. What's great about borrowing from Preston Browning's collection is that some of the books are annotated. Not only did I have books by the bed, but I had the professor's notes.

I found myself unable to put down *Wuthering Heights*, even in the dark hours of an old carriage house built in the early 19th century. I must say it was surely eerie entertaining Cathy's ghost, not to mention the complicated Heathcliff (ah, the poor "gipsy brat" reduced to an "it" brought home by Earnshaw, "the gift back to his children from Liverpool…, not a fiddle, not a whip, but instead...a gift of God…almost as if *it* came from the devil…"[italics mine]).

I also read **Charlotte Bronte**'s intro to her sister's book for a kind of footing, to be grounded in blood, as I had taught *Jane Eyre* and remembered the serial deaths Charlotte lived through. Charlotte and Emily both lived very closely under the specter of illness and death, and the reader of these Victorian novels must be ready and willing to swim in the often melodramatic dark waters. I had been reading my share of the men—namely **Roth** and **Dostoyevsky**—so I thought—yes give me the waters of the Bronte sisters—to balance all the misogyny that I have otherwise entertained myself with.

Instead of sleeping, I read through the night, listening to the old house creak and imagining my own ghosts in the atmosphere that seemed much transformed. When I saw, in the morning, the dull glow of ancient green, the leafy trees resembling moss outside my window, I felt almost sick, thick and dying with the story. The Cathy and Heathcliff of it, the song of Kate Bush running through my mind like an electrified current. Done, now for at least another twenty years?

Both *Brave New World* and *Wuthering Heights* came with second introductions—in the case of *Wuthering Heights* by the author's sister. I read **Huxley**'s second introduction, where he tells us that if he had to do it over again, there would be more than a passing mention of nuclear issues. I read this with a grim feeling, now that we are paying greater attention than we did two years ago to the escaping radiation from the fallen nuclear facility at Fukushima.

Tolstoy's collected stories titled *The Death of Ivan Ilyich and Other Stories*, where I read "Kreutzer Sonata" and "The Death…" I'm simply spellbound by these stories. In the latter, I marveled at Tolstoy's pacing, the depth of his characterization, the way his characters try to hide their antipathy, their selfishness, revealing themselves at each turn, not so unlike us now, as if death itself were contagious. Tolstoy's unsparing light into human pettiness and narcissism; with this hard light, he finds compassion, guiding us to salvation, as it were, watching Ilyich painfully enter his interior, in a never-too-late search for meaning, as he slips into the space where death cannot defeat him. And then in the "Kreutzer Sonata," another story where there is a death, but not so much redemption, where the hero would seem to make a religion out of misogyny—and still garner our sympathy. Responding to the suffering and the sacrifice of the woman in "Kreutzer…", I come away thinking: I must read more women, I must read more women, I must read more women.

MATTHEW O'BRIEN

Matthew O'Brien is an author and journalist who has lived in Las Vegas since 1997. His first book, *Beneath the Neon: Life and Death in the Tunnels of Las Vegas*, chronicles his adventures in the city's underground flood channels. His second book, *My Week at the Blue Angel: And Other Stories from the Storm Drains, Strip Clubs, and Trailer Parks of Las Vegas*, is a creative-nonfiction collection set in off-the-beaten-path Vegas. He's the founder of a community project that provides housing, drug counseling, and other services to the people living in the drains, and is currently enrolled in UNLV's master of fine arts creative-writing program.

http://www.beneaththeneon.com/

At the urging of my friend Chip Mosher, and being from the South and feeling somewhat obligated, I spent months reading *The Heart Is a Lonely Hunter* by **Carson McCullers**. Obviously, I didn't find it to be a page turner in the traditional sense. But it has a unique setting (a Georgia mill town in the 1930s), eccentric characters (including the town drunk, an African-American doctor, and two mutes), and poetic writing. It felt more like an epic poem than a novel. I'd recommend it to anyone who values language over narrative (though it's far from plot-free).

I'm also picking my way through **Allen Ginsberg**'s *Collected Poems 1947-1997*. Obviously, he wrote some beautiful and thought-provoking poems, especially in the '60s. But my secondary thought about the collection is: Man, he really overused the word "cock."

I, of course, was once again blown away by "Howl." "Elegy for Neal Cassady," "Ode to Failure," and "Personal Ads," among others, also earned a clumsy asterisk (marking my favorites).

Here are a few more titles towering over my wicker nightstand, casting a shadow on the bookmarks below:

Waddie Mitchell, *Waddie's Whole Load: The Cowboy Poetry of Waddie Mitchell*. If you live in Nevada, you have to read some cowboy poetry (I promise I did not make up that title!).

Charles Bowden, *Blue Desert.* I discovered this collection of dispatches (at least that's what I think it is) in a used bookstore in Tucson. The blurb on the back by **Edward Abbey**, one of my favorite writers, was enough to convince me to buy it. This time, my instincts didn't lead me astray, as *Blue Desert* proved to be a potent mix of poetry, journalism, and essay. Indicative of the collection, "Tortoises" starts as a piece about the plight of the threatened desert species and ends as a meditation on the Southwest, the people drawn to the region, and the author himself.

William T. Vollmann, *The Rainbow Stories*. After a few people recommended Vollmann, I bought this collection.

Joel Blau, *The Visible Poor: Homelessness in the United States*. I've been fascinated with homelessness—its causes, fraternity, effects, etc.—since the late '80s, when I went to college in downtown Atlanta. Disappointingly, there seems to be a dearth of books on the subject. This one, according to my research (surfing the Net for an hour or so), is among the best.

Andre Agassi, *Open: An Autobiography.* An opportunity for me to learn more about Las Vegas and one of its favorite sons. Also, I understand that the former tennis star really trashes some people in it. Can't wait!

A few months after contributing to "Books by the Bed," I started UNLV's creative-writing program and have been unable to read *Waddie's Whole Load*, *The Rainbow Stories*, *The Visible Poor*, and *Open*. A different stack of books, more international in nature, replaced them on the nightstand. They included *Senselessness* by **Horacio Castellanos Moya** (highly recommended), *Toddler-Hunting & Other Stories* by **Kono Taeko** (highly recommended), and *After Dark* by **Haruki Murakami** (skip it and read *The Wind-Up Bird Chronicle* or *Kafka on the Shore*).

As summer fades, only one book sits on the stand: *Naked* by **David Sedaris**. But I'm taking another forms of fiction class in the fall and the reading list is eerie and intriguing: *American Gothic Fiction*, by **Alan Lloyd-Smith**, *American Gothic Tales*, by **Joyce Carol Oates**, *The Keep* by **Jennifer Egan**, *Beloved* by **Toni Morrison**, *The Turn of the Screw* by **Henry James**, and *Bartleby the Scrivener* by **Herman Melville**. Hopefully, I can report back on these titles in a future "Books by the Bed."

CHERYL OLSEN

The daughter of belated Dust Bowl refugees, Cheryl Olsen left Oklahoma for the West at an early age.

She grew up in northern California, not surrounded by books as so many of her peers, but rather a strong oral tradition. The many storytellers in her extended family engendered a love of language that led her—again belatedly—to become an avid reader as a young adult. Truth be told, she became a cheerleader (aka aerobics instructor) at 30. Beginning to see a pattern?

She graduated from UC Berkeley and started a graduate program in ed psych. But just as the maze-running rats were making her squirrely, she fell under the spell of Filipino writer N.V.M. Gonzalez and former Iowa Writers' Workshop acting director Robert Williams. Both proffered encouragement and she belatedly but happily closed the lab door and succumbed to the urge that had been flirting with her for years. She drove to Iowa City in a borrowed El Camino with bemused husband Eric in tow.

Cheryl wrapped up her MFA in 1975, and endured two more frigid Iowa winters and steamy Iowa summers while Eric belatedly finished his BA, then graduate degrees. She got a job writing student profiles and features on UI programs for *The Iowa Scene*. She was a pro. There was no turning back.

Resettled in California, Cheryl wrote scores of articles for publications including *Cosmopolitan, Via*, *Runner Magazine*, and others. She was an editor and writer at *City Sports Magazine* for many years, and a columnist for *Women's Sports and Fitness*. Other clients include Time Inc. Health, Summit Medical Center, and Words Without Borders, among others. She also taught college English for a number of years.

During their four-decade marriage, Cheryl and Eric have frequently written for the same publications and collaborated on literary projects, including their publishing company, BrightCityBooks. Knowing the scope of *We Wanted to Be Writers*, and anticipating her level of pre-publication involvement (crash course in indexing and web goddessing, anyone?), Cheryl opted not to be interviewed for the book. Underestimating what a great read it would turn out to be, she wishes she'd consented. Belatedly.

Ok, so this is a bit of a fudge, since all thirteen of her novels aren't by my bed. But we went to **Jane Smiley**'s reading of *Private Life* at Book Passage in Corte Madera this week and there was a lot that's share-worthy and it's all about books, so I didn't think you'd mind.

All the novels, and her four nonfiction books, were on display, and Jane set the irreverent tone for the night with a quick children's game of Duck, Duck, Goose, using the more grownup Sex, Sex, No Sex deliniations as she hovered over each title.

We found out that *Private Life* is based on her great-aunt and her great-aunt's husband, and that Rose Wilder Lane (**Laura Ingalls Wilder**'s daughter, who was her inspiration for the *Little House* series) was in turn Jane's inspiration for Dora, the main character's modern sister-in-law. No spoiler alert needed, we also learned that "in the Scandinavian tradition, things start out bad and get worse."

But wait, there's more. On her other books, Jane had this to say:

On *A Thousand Acres* (her Pulitzer-winning novel based on "King Lear"): In Shakespeare, the scene where Goneril and Regan are talking about the knights, the heartless possibility of taking over their father's powers, "I thought, 'why not?' I was always on the girls' side."

And: "As I was driving from Minneapolis to Ames, through desolate landscape and weather, I thought, 'I should set that Lear book here.'"

On *Greenlanders*: "I got a Fulbright to Iceland (nobody wants to go there)." She adored Old Norse sagas, End of Time sagas . . . "and here's one that happened!"

On *Charles Dickens*, her biography of **Charles Dickens**: While other biographers had taken a Freudian approach, working from childhood to the novels, Jane decided her job was to interweave his novels into his life. She considers *Our Mutual Friend* Dickens' greatest book.

On young adult books (she's written four): Writing YA is "unbelievably fun! I grew up on these girls' horse books. They're all about power," and how young girls negotiate it.

On research for various books: For *13 Ways of Looking at the Novel* she read 130 novels (but not critics, she was quick to add). For *A Thousand Acres*, she read the Wednesday agricultural section of the *Des Moines Register*. For *Horse Heaven*, she went to the race track, and wrote it off. For *Moo*, she gossiped with people at Iowa State about things like the kid who purportedly could pee across the interstate.

Asked when she knew she could write, Jane recounted the tale of giving "Jeffrey Forgive Me" (which would become her first published short story) to a friend on their way to a reading by another author. At the same time the presenting writer grew quiet, the friend who was reading Jane's story burst out laughing at a passage. Jane said, "That's when I knew I was a writer."

Cheryl's Second Post

For most book lovers, the holidays bring welcome relief—for once other people support our self-indulgent habit. Cheryl (@2bwriters) shares recent gifts and old favorites by her bed.

Jane Smiley, *Moo.* For a couple of reasons. I recently read *Private Life*, a good read for a San Francisco Bay Area resident (downright gripping). I was reminded of Jane's wit at our reading at Book Passage last month and wanted to prolong the fun. The *Moo* romp with the denizens of a Midwestern university should entertain virtually everyone with a sense of humor. But a word of caution to those who have taught college: Don't read *Moo* in public—others may find your uncontrollable laughter disturbing.

William Zinsser, *Writing About Your Life*. Zinsser's classic, *On Writing Well*, has been in print well over three decades. *Writing About Your Life* is showing rather than telling at its best. Zinsser's been in the game forever, knows everyone, has great yarns to spin, and does so in a highly entertaining manner. Along the way, he unveils the art of memoir.

Tim O'Brien, *The Things They Carried*. This is by my side of the bed because I got it as a gift for Eric on the high recommendation of Twitter friend and reviewer *par excellence* Harvey Freedenberg (@HarvF) only to discover Eric already had it (Ok, fess up; I *know* we can't be the only couple who does this).

Rebecca Rasmussen, *The Bird Sisters: A Novel*. Another Twitter friend (@thebirdsisters). This has been on my wish list since it came out and Santa finally caved. Then I found myself procrastinating starting it in anticipation of how sad I would be to finish it. (It's a chick thing). The life-long relationship of sisters—with secrets!—is a complex unfolding, handled with just the right number of "crumbs" along the way.

Mary Karr, *Lit: A Memoir*. Because *The Liar's Club* will forever resonate. Have only managed the prologue so far, an open letter to her son. But it's predictably devastating and surprisingly funny and inexplicably grab-you-by-the-scruff-of-the-neck/shake-the-stuffing-out-of-you-and-never-let-go compelling. **(@marykarrlit)**

Leslie Brody, *Irrepressible: The Life and Times of Jessica Mitford*. A Christmas gift from Eric, who looked long and hard to find a memoir that wasn't too bleak to bear. Suspect he fell for Mitford's attribution as coiner of the term "frenemies."

Susannah Gardner and **Shane Birley**, *Blogging for Dummies*. Because I need all the help I can get.

ERIC OLSEN

Eric Olsen was born and raised in Oakland—*go A's!*—California and started college as a pre-med student at UC Berkeley, like all ambitious young freshmen at the time. His interest in medicine lasted about half-way through his first quiz in "orgo." He finished college many years and false starts later with a BA in Comparative Literature (Classical Greek, a long story and we won't get into that here). He got his MFA in fiction in 1977.

With Glenn Schaeffer, he co-founded in 2000 and then directed the International Institute of Modern Letters, a literary think tank that helped writers who were victims of censorship and persecution. Eric also helped establish the first American City of Asylum, in Las Vegas, an Institute program. The Institute also ran programs to support emerging writers in this country and abroad.

Before that, Eric was executive editor of custom publishing at Time Inc Health, a TimeWarner company. He left TimeWarner after that company's disastrous merger with AOL—in other words, too late. And before that, he was a freelance journalist.

Over the years, he has written hundreds of magazine articles and a few short stories, and written or co-written six nonfiction books, including *We Wanted to Be Writers*. He continues, despite common sense and the advice of concerned family and friends, to work on a novel and screenplay. Eric does sometimes wish he'd toughed it out in orgo.

Some of the books by my bed are there because I think I ought to read them, and there are books by my bed that I *want* to read. Some of the books by my bed are both. The books I keep by my bed that I think I *ought* to read are mostly nonfiction and very thick. I figure if I read them, I'll learn something. The books I *want* to read are generally cheap paperback crime novels. I figure they'll entertain me, and since I'm always trying to write a cheap paperback crime novel of my own—when I'm not trying to write a cheap paperback historical novel—I figure I'll learn something from them, too.

Niall Ferguson, *The War of the World: Twentieth Century Conflict and the Descent of the West*. Who says subtitles don't sell books? I bought this one precisely because of that "descent of the West." I'm a big fan of what is sometimes called "disaster porn," a sucker for anything declaring the end of this or the end of that, whether that end is brought on by environmental catastrophe, economic catastrophe, an asteroid the size of Kansas, a virulent new virus, zombies, giant lizards from outer space, even more Republicans in Congress, or, in the case of Ferguson's book, a sort of inevitable Malthusian catastrophe punctuated with RPGs, roadside bombs, and backpacks filled with gunpowder and nails, all worsened by a failure on the part of a fat, complacent West to think much beyond the next quarterly financial statement. At 600-plus pages, it's a bit of a slog, especially after a long day, but nonetheless a damned good read if you're into warnings about the collapse of everything. My wife has suggested on more than one occasion that I seek professional help…

And since we're on the topic, let me recommend a couple other works in the disaster porn genre, though neither is by my bed at the moment. One is **Anthony Pagden's** *Worlds at War: The 2,500-Year Struggle Between East and West*, and need I say that Pagden thinks the West is losing? The other is **Samuel P. Huntington's** *The Clash of Civilizations and the Remaking of World Order*, and again, goodbye West.

Update: Not long ago, Ferguson really stepped in it. He had his own Mitt Romney, 47-percent moment. Speaking to an audience of investors and financial analysts in California in early 2013, he said that John Maynard Keynes advocated for government spending to stimulate jobs during economic downturns because he was a homosexual and didn't have children and so didn't think long-term. Needless to say, Ferguson is no fan of Keynes nor his theories. Later, Ferguson offered "an unqualified apology" on his own website (http://www.niallferguson.com/blog/an-unqualified-apology). One does have to wonder what it is about audiences full of investors and analysts that brings out the stupid in folks.

Philip Kerr, *Berlin Noir*. This is three novels collected into one volume. They all feature the ex-police detective Bernie Gunther of Berlin. The first, *March Violets*, takes place in Berlin in 1936; the second, *The Pale Criminal*, in 1938; and the third, *A German Requiem*, in 1947. These are perfect novels for anyone with a fondness for disaster porn. I mean, we're talking Hitler, Gestapo, genocide, bombs, intrigue, spies, and one decent guy doing his best in evil times.

Walter Isaacson, *Einstein: His Life and Universe*. I came of age reading science fiction, so I've always had a thing about quantum theory and all that sort of stuff. This particular biography delves deeply into the creative process by which Einstein developed his theories, the influences in Einstein's life that perhaps helped foster his creative approach to the study of space and time, and Einstein's views on the links between freedom and creativity. I think it's a great read for anyone with an interest in Einstein and his theories of space and time, or an interest in the creative process in general.

Umberto Eco, *The Name of the Rose*. I love this one. I first read it not long after it was published in English—though long enough after it was first published that I found a used hardback in Moe's Books on Telly in Berkeley—and every now and then I read it again. It is, in the broadest sense, Sherlock Holmes set in an Italian monastery in 14th century Italy, with William of Baskerville, a tall, skinny Franciscan monk, as Sherlock Holmes, and Adso of Melk, a young Benedictine novice, William's scribe and assistant, as Dr. Watson. The tale is told by Adso. The book is long, dense, and great fun. William and Adso solve murders, wander around in a library that's a sort of Borgesian maze, and have lengthy discussions on religion, politics, philosophy, and more. Plus Adso has sex. What's not to like? The film made from the book, staring Sean Connery as William and a young Christian Slater as Adso, is also terrific.

John Irving, *The Cider House Rules*. Another of my favorites, which I re-read periodically, always asking myself, "How does he do it?" This book serves as a sort of antidote to all the disaster porn I'm always reading, as it's a tale of good people trying to do the Right Thing, though sometimes their attempts don't work out. It tells the story of Homer Wells, an orphan who grew up in St. Cloud's Orphanage in Maine. The main action is set around World War II. Homer doesn't get the girl, but (spoiler alert!) the ending is still rather upbeat.

Anthony Bukoski, *Polonaise* and *North of the Port*. Tony was one of my classmates at the Iowa Writers' Workshop. I got to know him first through the Friday Afternoon Boxing Club, where I was rather too often at the receiving end of one of his hard left hooks. Later, I became a big fan of his writing. I've never been much for short stories, whether writing them or reading them, but I find Tony's crisp, bare-knuckle prose and stories of the north woods endlessly appealing. I hear he's now working on a novel. I can't wait.

John Burdett, *Bangkok 8*. The first in a series of novels set in Bangkok and featuring the Royal Thai Police detective Sonchai Jitpleecheep, the son of a black American soldier and a Bangkok madam who, in partnership with Jitpleecheep's boss, opens a brothel that caters to aging American men on Viagra. Meanwhile, Jitpleecheep investigates the murders of his partner and a U.S. Army sergeant. Along the way, we learn about the jade and drug trades, sex, and Buddhism. Jitpleecheep also carries on a number of conversations with the ghost of his partner. I think it's a great novel to read in particular if you're interested in how to write about another culture. I thought the books that followed seemed a little more contrived. But *Bangkok 8*, at least, is a must-read.

Rick Atkinson, *Army at Dawn*. This is the first volume in a three-volume account of the Allied campaign in North Africa and Italy during World War II. This first volume covers the years 1942 through 1943, and comes complete with a photo of my old man as a young man—*quelle surprise*!—among a group of fellow Army cryptanalysts on a ship just prior to landing in Morocco. They're getting their heads shaved, as initiation into the Bald-Head Club. According to the caption, all the soldiers were ordered to shower before the invasion to reduce the risk of infection from wounds.

Isaiah Berlin, *The Proper Study of Mankind*. All of the essays in this collection serve in various ways as an antidote to all that disaster porn I'm so fond of. In these essays, Berlin takes on Big Ideas such as liberty, historical inevitability, and Tolstoy. Of an evening, I'll usually start with some Berlin, because I think it's good for the soul to read Berlin. But I can handle Berlin for only about five minutes at bedtime, so then I'll pick up one of the other books or one of the several stale issues of *The New Yorker* or *Atlantic* and try to finish one of the several articles I started weeks ago but never quite got through because I'd always fall asleep. And then I'll fall asleep…

Eric's Second Post

I'm currently trying to write an historical novel, and so by my bed right now are two excellent examples of the genre, **Ken Follett**'s *The Pillars of the Earth* and its sequel, *World Without End*. Granted, they probably wouldn't be considered "literature" by reviewers at the *New York Times*, but who cares? They're great reads.

They tell an engaging story simply, in simple language that I find particularly appropriate for late-night reading, when my brain's largely fried. The two novels together—2,000 pages of small type—tell the stories of several generations of people living in and around Kingsbridge, in England, from the 12th through the 14th centuries. The anchor for the tales is the building of a cathedral in Kingsbridge. The cathedral itself functions rather like a character, as it endures threats and defeats, rising slowly through the decades in fits and starts, the heart of a community.

Also by my bed is **Elizabeth Kostova**'s *The Historian*, to be read. It's not exactly an historical novel, since it's set more or less in the present day, but there are flashbacks, as well as vampires. I don't plan to read Kostova's novel for the vampires. Rather, I'm interested in seeing how Kostova constructs a story around flashbacks. My novel's going to have flashbacks, too, but no vampires, though I guess that runs counter to market forces these days and if I had any sense, I'd throw some in. Zombies, too. But Follett's novels are also devoid of vampires, as such. They are, rather, full of kings and church officials who act like vampires in the way they prey on the peasants.

ROBERT PEAKE

Robert Peake first came to our attention as one of the poets featured in *New Poets, Short Books*, a series published by Lost Horse Press and edited by Marvin Bell. We ran Marvin's inspirational intros to the five volumes last May. Robert's work has appeared in *North American Review*, *Poetry International*, *Rattle*, and other publications.

Now across The Pond, Robert writes about poetry and culture on *The Huffington Post* and runs the Transatlantic Poetry on Air online reading series, pairing poets from both sides of the Atlantic. His latest short collection, *The Silence Teacher*, was just published by Poetry Salzburg.

http://www.robertpeake.com/

A native Californian, I relocated to London with my English wife in spring 2011. Since it costs as much or more to ship a book that distance as it does to buy one new, we downsized considerably. Here are the few, which for financially irrational reasons, made the trip.

First, The Tomes, whose combined weight I don't even want to think about:

These include *A Handbook to Literature*, edited by **Hugh Holman** and **William Harmon**; *The Oxford Book of American Poetry*, chosen and edited by **David Lehman**; and *The Norton Anthology of Poetry*, edited by **Margaret Ferguson, Mary Jo**

Salter, and **Jon Stallworthy**.

I didn't take any of the three *Complete Works of Shakespeare* I had accumulated since college. But my MFA graduation present was a conveniently portable CD-ROM version of the *Oxford English Dictionary*, which my wife and I still use constantly to settle etymological scores.

The Big 'Uns, clocking in at over one-inch across the spine:

John Rember, *MFA in a Box: A Why to Write Book.* A kind of Boy Scout Field Guide for how to live as a writer, go deep in a shallow world, and not only survive in this wilderness, but (artistically) thrive.

Marvin Bell, *Nightworks: Poems 1962-2000*. The voice of my mentor and friend has been a constant source of inspiration and comfort through the dark winter months. I also admit to having convinced myself that *Stars Which See, Stars Which Do Not See*; *Wednesday: Selected Poems, 1966-1997*; and *These Green-Going-to-Yellow* were all slim enough not to count in my luggage. I am glad I did, as they are perfect for perusing on an overcrowded Tube commute.

Mark Doty, *Fire to Fire: New and Selected Poems*. This one got me through some dark times as well with its unflinching look at loss and hope.

The Urtexts (as in seminal or definitive):

Blake Morrison, editor, *The Penguin Book of Contemporary British Poetry*. This has served like a surveyor's map to this new literary landscape.

Czeslaw Milosz, *The Witness of Poetry*. Still one of the most insightful views on not only twentieth-century poetry, but the twentieth century itself.

The Contemporary Stuff:

Jane Hirshfield, *Given Sugar, Given Salt*. Defines a kind of quiet, Zen poem I still find deeply nourishing.

John Ashbery, *Some Trees*. It caused me to sit up and wonder, "How does he do that?" on first read, and remains a great source of pleasure on re-reading.

B.H. Fairchild, *The Art of the Lathe*. Spoke deep into my own Midwest ancestry, and showed me that a narrative poem can still be capable of stunning imagery and metaphor.

Charles Simic, *Selected Poems 1963-2003*. This haunted me with its European strangeness, and still gives me shivers today.

Sandra Alcosser, *A Fish to Feed All Hunger*. A slim but delicious early work from a voice I love to hear in my head.

Jonathan Harris, *The Wave That Did Not Break (The Ash Tree Poetry)*. The brave debut of a remarkable friend, face-to-face with his mother's suicide.

Michelle Bitting, *Good Friday Kiss*. Another good friend's powerhouse debut.

Sarah Maclay, *Music for the Black Room*. Startlingly sensuous, bordering on noir. Reading this on the Underground, I kept looking over my shoulder.

The Classics:

A little hardbound *Everyman's Library Pocket Poets* edition of **Gerard Manley Hopkins**, given to me as a graduation present by my mother. His rhythms still delight me like a jack-in-the-box. And **Neruda**'s *Captain's Verses: Love Poems*, with my own furious scribblings where I carried on arguments with the translator.

The ones in storage that I miss terribly:

Joseph Millar, *Overtime*. In the spirit of Fairchild and perhaps Levine, paying homage to hard work and sweet inner music.

David St. John, *Study For The World's Body: New and Selected Poems*. Another remarkably sensuous collection with a strong European feel.

And then there are several slim volumes of **Li-Young Lee** that used to make me hold my breath.

Irrational as it was, I'm glad I took these real books with me. E-books, although portable, are still abysmal for contemporary poetry. And as much as online developments help me feel connected to friends and family, when I want to plug in to the millennia-old tradition of poetry, there is nothing quite like having these pages to turn.

LYNNE PEREDNIA

Lynne Perednia is sysop and book reviewer at CompuServe Books & Writers Community, the oldest continually operating book forum on the Net. She's also a middle school librarian in a Title I school. Her book reviews are archived at Lynne's Book Notes, and she writes a weekly column on Contemporary Fiction Views at a well-known political website. She is active in the Washington Library Media Association and her local union, and occasionally fleshes out segments of the short story ideas in her chapbook.

http://lynne-booknotes.blogspot.com/
http://community.compuserve.com/Books

Evening reading is a full third of my day and keeps me inspired for the other hours. Reading is a solace and more rejuvenating than half a pot of three-day-old coffee, sometimes as bitter but more often a way to look at the day's challenges from a different perspective and know that there is a greater world out there waiting for all of us to discover. I have tried, but literally cannot sleep in a room without books.

Short stories are perfect for bed reading. You can get to the end of one story and put the book down to let the story sink in; short stories deserve this and more people deserve to read short stories. **Aimie Bender**'s *The Color Master* and **Claire Vaye Watkins**'s *Battleborn* have been particularly rewarding bedtime reads. Otherwise, a book like **Tash Aw**'s *Five Star Billionaire* will keep me going past curfew because I want to read just one more section. *Skippy Dies* by **Paul Murray** was a read like this and I ended up liking it far better than anticipated. Do not read **Joe Hill**'s remarkable *NOS4A2* in bed. You'll either get to a creepy part or want to keep reading; either way, it is not a restful-night-inducing book but one that I was glad to have read—even as someone who doesn't read much horror.

The headboard is a bookcase, and is filled with mysteries (to review or just because) such as *The Confession* by **Charles Todd** (set in post-WWI Britain as part of a favorite series); *The Darkest Room* by **Johan Theorin** (one of the brooding Scandinavian crime authors I adore); *Raylan* by **Elmore Leonard**; and older novels I meant to read or finish earlier, such as *Stone Arabia* by **Dana Spiotta** (which, with its theme of memory is proving a good follow-up to **Julian Barnes**'s *The Sense of an Ending*); and *Swamplandia!* by **Karen Russell** (moved closer to the top because of the Pulitzer snub).

Also residing there are books by the wisest women I would

wish to know, **Flannery O'Connor**'s collected works, *Gilead* and *Home* by **Marilynne Robinson** and **George Eliot**'s *Middlemarch*. These are the books I dip into the way other readers sample the Psalms and other poetry.

An occasional table beside the bed has the most immediate reading, including YA novels to review: *The Rock of Ivanore* by **Laurisa White Reyes**, **Roddy Doyle**'s *A Greyhound of a Girl*, and **Cynthia Leitich Smith**'s *Diabolical*—and the top layer of other books to review. These include **A.S. Byatt**'s *Ragnarok* (which I will treat as a companion piece to *The Children's Hour*, which was abandoned for some newly arrived shiny object, a.k.a. book), *The Unfinished Work of Elizabeth D*. by **Nichole Bernier**, *The Map and the Territory* by **Michel Houellebecq, Gregg Allman's** memoir, *My Cross to Bear*, **Christopher Moore**'s *Sacre Bleu!*, **Hari Kunzru**'s *Gods Without Men*, and **Edward St. Aubyn**'s *At Last*.

The bottom shelf of the table is filled with back issues of *The New Yorker*, *Times Literary Supplement* and *New York Review of Books* that I promise to recycle when read.

And if I ever go through all of these, there are six six-shelf bookcases of double-stacked mysteries in the room.

ANNE MARIE RUFF

Anne Marie Ruff, a published author and former journalist, currently works as an editor for a leading global law firm. Her work has been broadcast by NPR, BBC, PRI and International Herald Tribune TV, and published by *Time*, *The Christian Science Monitor*, and *Saveur* among other publications. Her first novel, *Through These Veins*, available in print and audio, was published in 2011 by Open Door Press. Absolute Certainty Entertainment optioned the film rights in 2013. Drawn from her extensive travels and the unique people she has met, *Through These Veins* brings together the disparate worlds of Ethiopia and AIDS/HIV research, and features two strong women in pursuit of a long-awaited cure. Her novel-in-progress, *Beneath the Same Heaven*, explores love, revenge and terrorism.

http://www.annemarieruff.com/

Most of my books by the bed arrive there as gifts from others, and most are nonfiction. Novels also arrive as gifts or recommendations, but these I carry religiously with me to read on my commute to and from the office and then pass them on once I am finished. I also end up with a number of books—memoirs, poetry, or novels—written by friends or relatives (what a wonder are the new publish-on-demand services).

Paulo Coelho, *The Fifth Mountain*. I will drop this into my Little Free Library without a recommendation, and stick to remembering Coelho for his brilliant *The Alchemist*.

Zadie Smith, *On Beauty*. A Christmas gift from two years ago still waiting to be read.

N.I. Vavilov, *Five Continents*. One of my heroes, Vavilov was a brilliant Russian agricultural scientist who collected crop seeds on five continents. Vavilov and E.O. Wilson have inspired in me a great passion for biodiversity. After Vavilov gave rise to the modern science of crop breeding and increasing crop yields, Stalin sent him to a gulag where he died of starvation. I have carried his book of field notes with me to four continents; maybe someday I will get to South America.

Henry David Thoreau, *Faith in a Seed*. For sentimental reasons I have kept this gift from my mother with me for nearly 20 years.

Bill Moyers, *Healing and the Mind*. Who can deny Moyers' premise that our own thinking and outlook impact the health or illness of our bodies?

Kathryn Stockett, *The Help*. A Christmas gift from last year. As good as everyone says it is.

Madame Romaine de Lyon, *The Art of Cooking Omelettes*. A little gem of a book, published in the 1960s, arrived as a gift from a friend when she heard I had acquired a flock of hens. Here's the secret to a good omelette—plenty of butter.

Aquila Ismail, *Of Martyrs and Marigolds*. A Pakistani friend's brave, recently published novel about the ugly division of East and West Pakistan into Bangladesh and Pakistan.

Saudi Aramco World Magazine. I am always stunned at the quality of writing and breadth of topics in this freely distributed piece of Middle Eastern petro-corporate goodwill.

Blake Snyder, *Save the Cat Goes to the Movies: The Screenwriter's Guide to Every Story Ever Told*. A fascinating deconstruction of the storyteller's arc.

How to Speak Punjabi. I still haven't learned after ten years, but I do know lots of slang not in the book, thanks to my Punjabi husband.

Tim Butcher, *Chasing the Devil: A Journey Through Sub-Saharan Africa in the Footsteps of Graham Greene*. After reading of his hike through Sierra Leone and Liberia, I feel no need to endure those miles myself.

Dale Ruff, *Walter Ruff: A Tribute to My Father*. My cousin's biography of my father's eldest brother and his life in North Dakota.

Lola Ruff, *Called by Name... Called to Serve*. My cousin's wife's memoir.

Vikram Chandra, *Red Earth and Pouring Rain: A Novel.* I finally dove into this book after it had sat in my pile for far too long. An incredible novel, with an ingeniously framed story and an epic sweeping arc.

Eric Olsen and **Glenn Schaeffer**, *We Wanted To Be Writers.* Of course!

FRED SETTERBERG

Fred Setterberg is the author of *Lunch Bucket Paradise: A True-Life Novel* and *The Roads Taken: Travels Through America's Literary Landscapes*, winner of the AWP prize in creative nonfiction. He and **Lonny Shavelson** co-authored *Under the Dragon: California's New Culture* and *Toxic Nation: The Fight to Save Our Communities from Chemical Contamination*. He lives in Oakland, California.

http://www.fredsetterberg.com/

These mornings, my wife Ann and I dip into *The Poets Laureate Anthology*, edited by **Elizabeth Hun Schmidt**, reading aloud over coffee selected morsels by **William Stafford**, **Maxine Kumin**, **Elizabeth Bishop**, and **Ted Kooser** (Ann, like Kooser, hails from Nebraska). As an alternative, we've been finishing off Wisconsin poet **Pamela Gemin**'s earthy, funny, winningly musical collection, *Another Creature*. She's terrific, and more people should know about her. We also loved **Steve Kowit**'s collection, *The Dumbbell Nebula.*

If only it would rain hard, and very long, I might get past the first chapter in *Alexander Hamilton* by **Ron Chernow**. I like to wrap myself up in big, fat histories during the long, cold, wet evenings of winter. (Last year, I finally tackled **Simon Schama**'s *Citizens: A Chronicle of the French Revolution*, after carting it around for a third of my life.) I drilled through Chernow's *The House of Morgan* at the start of the financial meltdown in 2008, and thought Hamilton might nicely bookend the crisis. Guess it'll have to wait for worse weather and better times.

I've been reading **Zola**, buying dog-eared paperback editions in our local independent bookstores. (Thank you, Oakland's Walden Pond, Spectator Books, and Book Zoo.) Soon I will have to choose between *Earth*, *Nana*, and *The Belly of Paris* for my next installment in the Rougon-Macquart series.

Although it's normally assigned to high school sophomores, I just finished reading *The Ox-Bow Incident* by **Walter Van Tilburg Clark**. That's led to listening in my car to the CD rendition of *The Last Gunfight: The Real Story of the Shootout at the O.K. Corral*—and *How It Changed the American West* by **Jeff Guinn**. (Guinn has just published a bio of Charles Manson, bringing new light to Californian criminality. I hope to see it on my bookstand soon.) The previous book I listened to was **Keith Richards**' *Life*, inexplicably read in alternating passages by Johnny Depp, Joe Hurley, and the man himself. Twenty CDs wasn't nearly enough.

To move from the figurative bedside to an actual piece of furniture, I continue to keep within grasp my childhood collection of Hardy Boys mysteries, the unearthly exploits of space cadet Tom Corbett, and the best, but least known of boys' adventure tales, the Rick Brant series by **John Blaine**. I last read *The Lost City*, about Rick's explorations in Tibet, to my godson Patrick when he was 11 or so. He turns 22 next month. I think it may be time to re-read *Stairway to Danger* or *The Caves of Fear*.

WILLIAM SOUDER

Journalist and author William Souder lives and writes in Grant, Minnesota, which is far enough into the country that he gets to watch his neighbor cutting hay three or four times a summer, and where he can see five barns from his office window but still make out the Minneapolis skyline looking like Oz in the distance, and where it gets so dark at night that you can sometimes see the coyotes by starlight. *Under a Wild Sky*, his biography of the bird artist John James Audubon, was a finalist for the Pulitzer Prize. His most recent book is *On a Farther Shore*, a biography of Rachel Carson that was published by Crown in September 2012 on the 50th anniversary of Carson's *Silent Spring*.

https://www.facebook.com/williamsouderauthor

The book on the nightstand I'm engrossed in right now is **Robert Massie**'s thoroughly readable *Catherine the Great,* which is as intricate and seductive as a Russian novel. Atop the just-completed pile is *Hedy's Folly: The Life and Breakthrough Inventions of Hedy Lamarr, the Most Beautiful Woman in the World*, by **Richard Rhodes**. What I loved about this book—what I love about so many books—is the author's alertness to a great, untold story. Who knew that Hedy Lamarr, besides being an actress, was a weapons inventor whose work on a World War II torpedo developed the technology on which today's cell phones depend? Not me.

On deck is **Jonathan Franzen**'s *Freedom*, because it's about time I got to it and also because I love the way he bashes e-books and social media. I guess you could say I've got a bad attitude about certain things, which is, of course, essential for a writer. Franzen rails against the headlong digital evolution of books, which I think is inevitable and in some ways a terrible mistake. That presumably doesn't have anything to do with *Freedom*, but it ups my interest.

Here are some other titles by the bed—on what is actually *not* a nightstand per se, but rather a fairly good-sized book shelf:

Theodore Draper, *A Struggle for Power: The American Revolution.* The American Revolution well-told.

Richard Dawkins, *The Greatest Show on Earth: The Evidence for Evolution.* Evolution is the true sweet science. It would be a stretch to call it the "meaning" of life—but it's certainly the nature of it.

James Watson, *The Double Helix: A Personal Account of the Discovery of the Structure of DNA.* I'm always thinking about biology and might write something one day about what happened to it during the 20th century. I don't think any other branch of knowledge changed so profoundly in such a short span of time. In the early 1900s we had only a dim picture of what the inside of a living cell looked like. By the end of the millennium we had unlocked the cell's secrets—not all of them, but many—at the molecular level.

Bruce Alberts, et al. *The Molecular Biology of the Cell.* Like I said, this is a subject that fascinates me. All you need to make a living cell is a handful of light elements—hydrogen, oxygen, nitrogen, carbon, and phosphorous are a pretty good start. Devote a portion of the hydrogen and oxygen to a substrate—water—and you're in business. Inside a cell, these elements form the backbones of macromolecules that have remarkable properties of self-assembly and replication. The cell is nature's triumph of chemical organization. It is amazing. *Amazing.* Biologists say that while there is no precise definition of "life," one feature of all life on earth is its "emergent properties." In the same way that a pile of bricks becomes something more functional if turned into a wall (or even better, a room), a cell is more than the sum of its parts. A cell can also be, in the case of a fertilized egg, the blueprint for a complex organism consisting of many cells. Cells are us.

Christopher Hitchens, *Arguably: Essays.* There will never be another C.H., which I suppose is fine for the many people he drove bonkers. But I miss his wit, his sharp tongue, and his living proof that a well-read person is someone to be reckoned with.

Henry Beston, *The Outermost House: A Year of Life on the Great Beach of Cape Cod.* Because it's *Walden* for me, an American classic that far too few people have read. I only discovered this extraordinary book in the course of my research on Rachel Carson—it was one of her favorites. Whenever anybody asks me for a reading suggestion it's the first title I mention.

Last, but never least—and always found close at hand—is *The Sun Also Rises*. I don't think this requires any explanation.

DON WALLACE

Don Wallace was born in Long Beach, California. He wrote his way through UC Santa Cruz, then it was on to Iowa for an MFA in fiction from the Writers' Workshop in 1978 and marriage to fellow workshopper Mindy Pennybacker—to whom he was first introduced by Eric Olsen.

He worked for 26 years in Manhattan as a magazine editor at Hearst, Conde Nast, Time Inc, and The New York Times Magazine Group, becoming a specialist in startups, sports and leisure (*Yachting*, *Motorboating & Sailing*, *Golf Digest Woman*), business (*Fast Company*, *Success*), women's (*Self*, *Parents*), and other publications. In Honolulu, he was film editor of *Honolulu Weekly*, which

Mindy edited, and now is film and literary editor of *HI Spy*, a startup he and Mindy and a core group are currently publishing at *HI-Spy.Tumblr.com*, with plans for a website and print edition in the near future.

During his time in Manhattan he wrote fiction and memoirs, including the novel *Hot Water*, and *One Great Game*, about high school football. He also reviewed more than 100 novels, mostly debuts, in *Kirkus Reviews*, and taught fiction and creative nonfiction at The New School for Social Research and journalism at the graduate publishing program at Pace University.

His essays, op-eds, columns, reviews and articles have appeared in *Harper's*, *The New York Times*, MediaLifeMagazine.com, *The Green Guide*, *Fast Company*, *Naval History*, *Islands*, *Wine Spectator*, *Diversion*, *Robb Report*, and others. An essay on Baja California won the 1985 Pluma de Plata Mexicana for reporting on Mexico; a short story, "The Injunction," was a 2006 selection for *Next Stop Hollywood* (St. Martins). He also received the James Michener Prize from the Copernicus Society for a novel and the Elisabeth Mignon Puknat Poetry Award.

His greatest/strangest writing-related moment came on the occasion of receiving an author-of-the-year award from the U.S. Naval Institute, for his serialized novel *The Log of Matthew Roving*: He found himself addressing the Joint Chiefs of Staff of the U.S. Armed Forces, 25 foreign military attaches and several hundred Naval and Marine officers in 2002, at the U.S. Naval Academy, hours before the invasion of Baghdad.

He and Mindy now live in Honolulu, while their son, Rory, has taken up the baton in Manhattan. While settling in, Don wrote the documentary film, "Those Who Came Before: The Musical Journey of Eddie Kamae," about the 50-year search for the last remaining singers and composers of the ancient Hawaiian music. It is directed by Eddie Kamae, founder of the Sons of Hawaii, and Myrna

Kamae. He then wrote two different drafts of *Village Idiots* and performed a delicate surgery to join them into one memoir that will be published in 2014.

https://www.facebook.com/don.wallace.9674

Before Mindy took away my end table, the usual teetering stack included my classmate **Jennie Fields**' *The Age of Desire*, a novel of Edith Wharton's choices and love life—it's very good and as always with Wharton leaves me pondering how such a great writer could be so constrained by society. Then I look at myself and say, "*Touché*, baby." Another classmate's book, *The Forever War*, which I found at the Long Beach Jewish Community Center, also had a place in the stack. It's the third version, of which author **Joe Haldeman** approves.

Reaching down to the floor and letting my fingers do the walking, as they say, I fetch up *'68* by **Paco Ignacio Taibo II**. One of the great subversives, he does Mexican noir political fiction. I envy the Mexican writing circles; they give the impression of pals freely trading manuscripts and reading them, the ideal world we writers are always longing for, discussing books long into the night and smoking cigarettes. It's about the shootings in '68 in Mexico, when the Army let loose on student protestors in Mexico City's central plaza.

My hand recently closed around the Summer 2013 issue of *Lapham's Quarterly*, an anthology of texts about the sea. Lewis Lapham was my first editor-in-chief at *Harper's*, and his taste is impeccable here as well. Since in my mind I am a waterman, a tattooed harpoonist and a bowsprit dancer, anything about the sea revives me. This partially explains **Fred Waitzkin**'s new novel, *The Dream Merchant*, which starts, *Heart of Darkness*-style, in the dark off the coast of the Bahamas and proceeds to tell the episodic story of one of those charismatic bastards of capitalism that I ran into and wrote about when I was a nautical journalist.

Lastly, the pile of books about France is thick and yellow-flagged. I have been writing a book about this island in

Brittany that Mindy and I go to—and after 19 years of drafts I sold the sucker. *Village Idiots: How a Ruin They Couldn't Afford on a Tiny French Island Too Far from Home Renovated an American Family*. (Now *there's* an elevator pitch!) It should come out in June 2014 from Sourcebooks of Chicago (see DonWallaceFranceBlog.Tumblr.com).

Anyway, in this French pile by the bed there are books that inform my French pile: *The Old Regime and the Revolution* (**de Tocqueville**); *Belle-Ile-en-Mer: Histoire d'une Ile* (**Louis Garans**); and *Belle Ile Vagabondages* (**Michel Benech**, **Etienne Lebigre**, and **Paul Mauger**), a compendium of island fauna, flora, geology, geography, and history arranged by long, invigorating walks. The latter goes particularly well with a Macallans 12-year-old (can't afford the 18-year-old) while slouched in a wicker basket chair.

Don's Second Post

The addition of a Kindle on each side of the bed has reduced some of the clutter, but not as much as you'd expect. For one thing, you can't read the screen in the dark and one of us knocks out pretty much as soon as she goes horizontal. But the portable impulse-buying device has allowed me to put the digital equivalent of 5,000 pages on a shaky night table without bringing it any closer to collapse.

Speaking of collapse, that's the second book I finished on my Kindle: *Collapse: How Societies Choose to Fail or Succeed* by **Jared Diamond**. It's perfect for Hawaii, which shudders ever closer to the precipice, replicating the barnblindism of the people of Greenland, Easter Island, Pitcairn Island…

The first book I finished was the *Personal Memoirs of Ulysses S. Grant*. It's advertised as the best of its kind, but I'd add the caveat, "If you like detailed, laconic descriptions and pithy summaries of complicated battles fought under nasty inclement conditions and against a relentless foe: human stupidity and fecklessness and vaingloriousness." I do. Like it, that is.

Along with **Jennifer Egan**'s *A Visit from the Goon Squad* (highly recommended) and the as-yet unstarted *'68* by **Paco Ignacio Taibo II**, we have **Patti Smith's** *Just Kids*—both digital and in a real book. (The book is winning the who's-more-popular battle: It's just a cool object, wrapped in black, like Patti Smith herself.) And I do have a bookmark stuck halfway through **David McCullough**'s book about writers and artists in France, *The Greater Journey*. It's broad-stroke stuff but I enjoy wading in the subject matter and dreaming of our own return to France.

I also read **Kaui Hart Hemmings**' *The Descendants* after seeing the movie (Mindy did a series of interviews), having met and liked her. Also, having recognized the people she was writing about, some of whom I know or knew. The movie is very good; the novel, too, but even more surprising in how she handles the back-story and "exotic" locale by, essentially, not going there. This is a liberating strategy for those of us who feel an obligation to put a place on the map and get it right. She got it right by not trying to explain everything or to include everybody. This has exposed her to some criticism that the book is only about and for the slice of upper-crust Hawaiian-missionary society that has shaped Hawaii and still exerts unholy influence.

But, to me, that's like saying Shakespeare's plays are only about kings and queens and aristocrats and therefore to be relegated to Marx's dustbin of history. To reinforce the point, I'm reading **Julia Flynn Siler**'s *Lost Kingdom: Hawaii's Last Queen, the Sugar Kings, and America's First Imperial Adventure*. It's a big explanatory book set at the moment of The Overthrow (of Queen Liliuokalani) and already in the first 20 pages has exhibited both the virtues and flaws of the popular encyclopedic narrative.

Next to that is our friend and Mindy's surf partner **Sydney Iaukea**'s *The Queen and I*, her just-published account of her disenfranchisement by her own family, despite being part of a royal Hawaiian line and seemingly in line to inherit a chunk of the vast estates passed down. While researching topics for her PhD dissertation, Sydney stumbled upon her own family's archives by accident; these included evidence of how her mother had been conned out of their share. The best revenge is writing, and Sydney's is superb.

ELLISON G. WEIST

Ellison G. Weist hails from a long line of bibliomaniacs. Her personal battle with the illness has led to her being labeled "The Book Bully" due to a tendency to approach total strangers in bookstores with the hopes of, yes, infecting them.

After a sales career with a "major soft drink company," Ellison spent three years as a book editor for a Portland, Oregon, newspaper. These days she enjoys matching readers with books; finding new spots to hide book purchases from her long-suffering husband; and blogging about books.

www.thebookbully.wordpress.com

Threats from my neat-freak husband have trimmed the number of books that reside on my bedside table. Since I am blessed with a man who enjoys dusting, I cannot complain. At least not while he's in the room.

I recently picked up *A Clash of Kings*, the second book in the *A Song of Ice and Fire* series by **George R.R. Martin**. Friends who know my reading tastes find this unfathomable since, on the whole, I cannot abide the fantasy genre. But there is something utterly addictive about these books. Martin's characters are fleshed out to the point where I can overlook the phantasmagoric elements that puzzle me.

An unfortunately small pile next to Martin's 700-page paperback holds several books I keep meaning to get to. These include the new novel by **Audrey Schulman**, *Three Weeks in December*, and the debut by **C.E. Morgan**, *All the Living*. I enjoyed Schulman's latest. It features two main characters divided by a century. In 1899, Jeremy, a disgraced engineer leaves his home in Maine to oversee the building of a railroad in the African bush. One hundred years later Max, an autistic researcher, heads to Rwanda in search of a rare vine that could be a pharmaceutical phenomena. Both stories are fascinating. My copy is published by Europa Editions. One reason I adore the Europa Edition books is how portable they are and how easy they are to handle in bed. For me, they're the perfect size to cuddle up with. Plus I'm a sucker for French flaps. I'm embarrassed to say how many Europa Edition books I've purchased simply because of their size and feel!

C.E. Morgan is from Kentucky. I'm getting ready to visit family back there so I may need to pack it. I'm also sniffing around *The Surrendered* by **Chang-rae Lee**; however, one friend described the first 30 pages of Lee's latest as "devastating," and that gives me pause. I still haven't read it. Every time I pick it up, I get a queasy feeling in the pit of my stomach and put it aside. What a wimp!

About a quarter of the space on my bedside table will always be occupied by a five-volume set of books by **Louisa May Alcott**: *Little Women, Little Men, Jo's Boys, Old-Fashioned Girl*, and *Eight Cousins*. These black calfskin-bound treasures originally belonged to my maternal grandmother and her older sister. I inherited them as a pre-teen and devoured all five over the period of a month. What I remember loving about these books was how busy all the characters were, how much "drama" they contained. As a child I was always drawn to stories that took place in what I called "the olden days," so Alcott's stories appealed to me for their content and setting.

I remember being fascinated by the fact that more than

fifty years earlier, two young girls from Kentucky had read and cherished these very same volumes. Because of the books' increasingly delicate condition—they're more than 100 years old—my own daughter was unable to read them, but I made sure to purchase her paperback copies. She, like all of her kinswomen, loved every tale.

Today each of these precious books is in need of rebinding. But until I find a professional I trust, they will remain by my side of the bed—as testaments to the love of reading that has sustained my family for generations.

I cannot read gore or horror before sleep. This dates back to my experience with *The Shining* by **Stephen King**. I read it the summer before my senior year in college and it scared me so badly I made my youngest brother sleep on my bedroom floor for about a week. This embarrassing little tidbit still comes up at family reunions.

BOOKS BY OUR CONTRIBUTORS

Jeffrey Abrahams

The Mission Statement Book: 301 Corporate Mission Statements from America's Top Companies (Ten Speed Press/Random House, 1995, now in its third edition)

Valerie Brooks

"*Liberté*," a short memoir, in *France: a Love Story; Women Write About the French Experience* (Seal Press/ Avalon Publishing, 2004)

"Dead Children" in *Scent of Cedars: Thirty-two Promising Writers from the Pacific Northwest* (Russell Dean & Company, 2002)

David Davis

Marathon Crasher: The Life and Times of Merry Lepper, The First American Woman to Run a Marathon (Thomas Dunne Books, 2012)

Showdown at Shepherd's Bush: The 1908 Olympic Marathon and the Three Runners Who Started a Running Craze (Thomas Dunne Books, 2012)

"The 13th Round" in *The Best American Sports Writing*, Glenn Stout, ed. (Houghton Mifflin, 1996)

"You Can't Spell Hate Without Hat" in *I Hate the Dallas Cowboys And Who Elected Them America's Team, Anyway*, Bert Sugar, ed. (St. Martin's Griffin, 1997)

"Marvin, Marvin" in *Basketball in America: From the Playgrounds to Jordan's Game and Beyond*, Bob Batchelor, ed. (Haworth Press, 2005)

Karin Evans

We're All Walking Home in the Dark, forthcoming novel

Not Quite Home, forthcoming poetry collection

The Grace to Race: The Wisdom and Inspiration of the 80-Year-Old World Champion Triathlete known as The Iron Nun (Simon & Schuster, 2010)

The Lost Daughters of China: Adopted Girls, Their Journey to America, and the Search for a Missing Past (Penguin/Tarcher, 2008)

Jennie Fields

The Age of Desire (Penguin, 2012)

The Middle Ages: A Novel (Harper Perennial, 2003)

Crossing Brooklyn Ferry (Harper Perennial, 2002)

Lily Beach (Grand Central Publishing, 1994)

Catherine Gammon

Sorrow (Braddock Avenue Books, 2013)

with Bruce Smith, editors, *Cape Discovery: The Provincetown Fine Arts Work Center Anthology* (Sheep Meadow, 1994)

Isabel Out of the Rain (Mercury House, 1991)

Joe Haldeman

Joe's first book is *War Year* (Holt, 1972). Since *War Year,* he's published more than 30 novels, including *The Forever War*, perhaps his best-known novel, released in 1974. (Joe's preferred version of that novel was issued by St. Martin's in 2009). Here are a few of Joe's most recent books:

Work Done for Hire (forthcoming, Ace Books, 2014)

Earthbound (Ace Books, 2011)

Starbound (Ace Books, 2010)

Marsbound (Ace Books, 2008)

The Accidental Time Machine (Ace Books, 2007)

Denise Hamilton

Damage Control (Scribner Reprint, 2011)

Prisoner of Memory (Scribner, 2006)

Savage Garden (Scribner, 2005)

Last Lullaby (Scribner Reprint, 2004)

The Last Embrace (Scribner, 2001)

Sugar Skull (Scribner, 2003)

The Jasmine Trade (Scribner, 2001)

as editor:

LA Noir 2 (Akashic Noir Series, 2013)

LA Noir (Akashic Noir Series, 2012)

Terry Johnson

with Kyle Kurpinski, *How to Defeat Your Own Clone: And Other Tips for Surviving the Biotech Revolution* (Bantam, 2010)

Victoria Johnson

The Doctor's Dilemma (Montlake Romance, 2011)

Grant Writing 101: Everything You Need to Start Raising Funds Today (McGraw-Hill, 2010)

The Substitute Bride (Amazon Digital Services, 2012)

Geri Lipschultz

"In the Beginning of the End" (poem) and "Slow Dance of the Heart" (story) in *Literature: An Introduction to Reading and Writing,* Edgar V. Roberts and Robert Zweig, eds. (Pearson Publishing, forthcoming)

"All Traces of the Fallacy Dawn" (story) in *The Wreckage of Reason: An Anthology of Xxperimental Prose by Women Writers* (Spuyten Duivil Press, forthcoming)

"To Everything There Is a Season: Or What to Expect When You're a Writer Expecting a Baby" and "Mother Professor: Going Back for the Ph.D." in *Women Writing on Family: Tips on Writing, Teaching and Publishing* (Key Publishing Company, 2012)

"What Remains of Hope" (poem) in *The Light of City and Sea: an Anthology of Suffolk County Poetry*, Daniel Moran, editor (Street Press, 2006)

with Peter Jay, translations from the Polish of poems by Ewa Lipska in *Voices Within the Ark: Modern Jewish Poets,* Anthony Rudolf and Howard Schwartz, eds. (Pushcart Press, 1980)

with Peter Jay, translation from the Polish of "Censored" by Ewa Lipska, in *Writing from the World*, Paul Engle and and Hua Ling Nieh Engle, eds. (University of Iowa Press, 1976)

Matthew O'Brien

My Week at the Blue Angel: And Other Stories from the Storm Drains, Strip Clubs, and Trailer Parks of Las Vegas (Huntington Press, 2010)

Beneath the Neon: Life and Death in the Tunnels of Las Vegas (Huntington Press, 2007)

Eric Olsen

with Glenn Schaeffer, *We Wanted to Be Writers: Life, Love, and Literature at the Iowa Writers' Workshop* (Skyhorse Publishing, 2011)

with Fu-Tung Cheng, *Concrete at Home: Innovative Forms and Finishes: Countertops, Floors, Walls, and Fireplaces* (Taunton Press, 2005)

with Fu-Tung Cheng, *Concrete Countertops: Design, Forms, and Finishes for the New Kitchen and Bath* (Taunton Press, 2002)

with Ralph Paffenbarger, M.D., *LifeFit: an Effective Exercise Program for Optimal Health and a Longer Life* (Human Kinetics Publications, 1996)

editor, *Forming a Moral Community* (Bioethics Consultation Group, 1995)

On the Right Track: A Viewer's Guide to 1984 Olympic Running Events (Bobbs-Merrill, 1984)

Robert Peake

The Silence Teacher (Poetry Salzburg, 2013)

Human Shade (Lost Horse Press, 2011)

Anne Marie Ruff

Through These Veins (Open Door Press, 2011)

Beneath the Same Heaven, forthcoming

Fred Setterberg

Lunch Bucket Paradise: A True-Life Novel (Heyday Books, 2011)

with Lonny Shavelson, *Under the Dragon: California's New Culture* (Heyday Books, 2007)

editor, *Travelers' Tales Guides—America: True Stories of Life on the Road* (Travelers' Tales, 1999)

The Roads Taken: Travels Through America's Literary Landscapes (The University of Georgia Press, 1998)

with Lonny Shavelson, and *Toxic Nation: The Fight to Save Our Communities from Chemical Contamination* (John Wiley & Sons, 1993)

William Souder

On a Farther Shore: The Life and Legacy of Rachel Carson (Crown, 2012)

Under a Wild Sky: John James Audubon and the Making of The Birds of America (North Point Press, 2004)

Plague of Frogs: The Horrifying True Story (Hyperion, 2000)

Don Wallace

Village Idiots: How a Ruin They Couldn't Afford on a Tiny French Island Too Far From Home Renovated an

American Family (Sourcebooks, forthcoming June 2014)

One Great Game: Two Teams, Two Dreams, in the First Ever National Championship High School Football Game (Atria Books, 2003)

A Tide in Time: The Log of Matthew Roving (Naval History, 2000-03)

Hot Water (Soho Press, 1991)

WaterSports Basics (Prentice-Hall, 1985)

BOOKS DISCUSSED BY OUR CONTRIBUTORS

A

Chris Abani, *Song for Night* (Akashic Books, 2007)

Chinua Achebe, *Things Fall Apart* (Anchor, 1994)

Chris Adrian, *The Great Night*, (Farrar, Straus and Giroux, 2011)

Bruce Alberts, et al. *The Molecular Biology of the Cell* by (Garland Science, 2007)

Sandra Alcosser, *A Fish to Feed All Hunger* (Ahsahta Press, 2011)

Louisa May Alcott: *Little Women, Little Men, Jo's Boys, Old-Fashioned Girl*, and *Eight Cousins* (The University Press, Cambridge, publication dates from 1914-1917)

Nelson Algren, *The Neon Wilderness* (Seven Stories Press, 2002)

Gregg Allman, *My Cross to Bear* (William Morrow, 2013)

Sherwood Anderson, *Death in the Woods and Other Stories* (Liveright, 2006)

Max Apple, *The Jew of Home Depot and Other Stories* (The Johns Hopkins University Press, 2007)

John Ashbery, *Some Trees* (ECCO Press, 1978)

Jay Asher, *Thirteen Reasons Why*, (Razorbill, 2011)

Rick Atkinson, *Army at Dawn* (Henry Holt, 2002)

Marcus Aurelius, *Meditations* (various editions, including the translation by Gregory Hays, Modern Library, 2002)

Tash Aw, *Five Star Billionaire* (Spiegel & Grau, 2013)

B

Blake Bailey, *A Tragic Honesty: The Life and Work of Richard Yates* (Picador, 2004)

Nicholas Baker, *The Anthologist* (Simon and Schuster, 2010)

Julian Barnes, *The Sense of an Ending* (Vintage Books, 2012)

Nicholas Basbanes, *Editions & Impressions: My Twenty Years on the Book Beat* (Fine Books Press, 2008)

Christopher Beha, *What Happened to Sophie Wilder* (Tin House Books, 2012)

Marvin Bell, *Nightworks: Poems 1962-2000* (Copper Canyon Press, 2003); *Stars Which See, Stars Which Do Not See* (Carnegie Mellon, 1992); *Wednesday: Selected Poems, 1966-1997* (Salmon Poetry, 1998); *These Green-Going-to-Yellow* (Atheneum Books, 1981); and editor, *New Poets, Short Books* (Lost Horse Press, 2011)

Aimi Bender, *The Color Master* (Doubleday, 2013)

Michel Benech, **Etienne Lebigre**, and **Paul Mauger**, *Belle Ile Vagabondages* (Maison de la Nature de Belle-Ile-en-Mer)

Chistopher Benfey, *A Summer of Hummingbirds* (Penguin Books Reprint, 2009)

Isaiah Berlin, *The Proper Study of Mankind* (Farrar, Strauss and Giroux, 2000)

Nichole Bernier, *The Unfinished Work of Elizabeth D.* (Broadway Books, 2013)

Henry Beston, *The Outermost House: A Year of Life on the Great Beach of Cape Cod* (Holt Paperbacks, 2003)

Kai Bird and **Martin J. Sherman**, *American Prometheus: The Triumph and Tragedy of J. Robert Oppenheimer* (Vintage Books, 2006)

Michelle Bitting, *Good Friday Kiss* (C&R Press, 2008)

John Blaine, *The Lost City* (Grosset & Dunlap, 1947); *Stairway to Danger* (Grosset & Dunlap, 1952); and *The Caves of Fear* (Aegypan, 2011)

Joel Blau, *The Visible Poor: Homelessness in the United States* by (Oxford University Press, 1993)

Francesca Lia Block, *Pink Smog* (Harper Teen, 2012)

Roy Blount, Jr., *Roy Blount's Book of Southern Humor* (W.W. Norton, 1994)

Charles Bowden, *Blue Desert* (University of Arizona Press, 1988)

T.C. Boyle, *World's End* (Penguin Books, 1990) and *When the Killing's Done* (Penguin Books, Reprint Edition, 2012)

Leslie Brody, *Irrepressible: The Life and Times of Jessica Mitford* (Counterpoint, 2010)

Charlotte Bronte, *Jane Eyre* (Wilder Publications, Reprint Edition, 2009)

Emily Bronte, *Wuthering Heights* (Dover, 1996)

Anthony Bukoski, *Time Between Trains,* (Holy Cow! Press, 2011)**;** *Polonaise* (Southern Methodist University Press, 1998); and *North of the Port* (Southern Methodist University Press, 2008)

John Burdett, *Bangkok 8* (Vintage, 2004)

Tim Butcher, *Chasing the Devil: A Journey Through Sub-Saharan Africa in the Footsteps of Graham Greene* (Atlas, 2011)

Blake Butler, *There Is No Year* (Harper Perennial, 2011)

A.S. Byatt, *Ragnarok* (Candlewick, 2013)

C

Ethan Canin, *America America* (Random House, 2009)

Vikram Chandra, *Red Earth and Pouring Rain: A Novel* (Back Bay Books, 1995)

Ron Chernow, *Alexander Hamilton* (Penguin Books, 2005) and *The House of Morgan* (Grove Press, 2010)

Walter Van Tilburg Clark, *The Ox-bow Incident* (Modern Library, 2004)

Paulo Coelho, *The Fifth Mountain* (Harper Perrenial, 2009) and *The Alchemist* (HarperCollins, 2006)

Jim Cohee, *The Swan* (Indiana University Press, 2011)

Billy Collins, *Ballistics: Poems* (Random House, 2010)

John Connolly, *The Infernals: A Samuel Johnson Tale* (Atria Reprint, 2012)

D

Dante, *The Inferno*, Robert and Jean Hollander, translators (Anchor, 2002)

Clarence Darrow, *The Story of My Life*, (Da Capo Press, 1996)

Richard Dawkins, *The Greatest Show on Earth: The Evidence for Evolution* (Free Press, reprint edition, 2010)

Lucille Lang Day, *The Curvature of Blue* by (Cervena Barva Press, 2009) and *Wild One* (Scarlet Tanager Books, 2000)

Kiran Desai, *Hullabaloo in the Guava Orchard* (Grove Press, 2009)

Peter Desberg and **Jeffery Davis,** *Show Me the Funny!: At the Writers' Table with Hollywood's Top Comedy Writers* (Sterling, 2010)

Jared Diamond, *Collapse: How Societies Choose to Fail or Succeed* (Penguin Books, 2011)

Charles Dickens, *Our Mutual Friend* (Oxford University Press, 2009)

E. J. Dionne, Jr., *Our Divided Political Heart: The Battle for the American Idea in an Age of Discontent* (Bloomsbury USA, 2012)

John Donne, *Batter My Heart* (Amazon Digital Services, Inc., 2012)

Mark Doty, *Fire to Fire: New and Selected Poems* (Harper Perennial Reprint Edition, 2009)

Roddy Doyle, *A Greyhound of a Girl* (Amulet Books, 2012)

Theodore Draper, *A Struggle for Power: The American Revolution* (Vintage, 1997)

Daphne du Maurier, *Rebecca* (William Morrow Paperbacks (2006)

E

Umberto Eco, *The Name of the Rose* (Harcourt Brace Jovanovich, 1983)

Jennifer Egan, *A Visit From the Goon Squad* (Anchor, 2011) and *The Keep* (Anchor, 2007)

Deborah Eisenberg, *Twilight of the Superheroes* (Picador, 2007)

George Eliot, *Middlemarch* (Penguin Classics, 2003)

T.S. Eliot, *Four Quartets* (Mariner Books, 1968)

Joseph Epstein, *Narcissus Leaves the Pool* (Mariner Books, 2007) and *In a Cardboard Belt! Essays Personal, Literary, and Savage* (Houghton Mifflin Harcourt, 2007)

F

B.H. Fairchild, *The Art of the Lathe* (Alice James Books, 1998)

William Faulkner, *The Viking Portable Faulkner* (Random House, 1985); *Go Down, Moses* (Vintage, 1973); *Absalom, Absalom!* (Modern Library, 1993); *The Sound and the Fury* (Modern Library, 1992)

Margaret Ferguson, Mary Jo Salter, and **Jon Stallworthy**, editors, *The Norton Anthology of Poetry* (5th ed., W.W. Norton, 2004)

Niall Ferguson, *The Ascent of Money: A Financial History of the World* (Penguin Books, 2009) and *The War of the World: Twentieth Century Conflict and the Descent of the West* (The Penguin Press, 2006)

David Ferry, translator, *The Odes of Horace*, (Farrar, Straus and Giroux, 1998)

Jasper Fforde,*The Eyre Affair: a Thursday Next Novel* (Penguin Books, 2003)

Jennie Fields, *The Age of Desire* (Pamela Dorman Books, 2012)

Marina Fiorato, *The Glassblower of Murano* (St. Martin's Griffin, 2011)

Ken Follett, *The Pillars of the Earth* (New American Library, 2007), and *World Without End* (NAL, 2008)

Richard Ford, *Canada* (Ecco, reprint edition, 2013)

John Fowles, *The Collector* (Back Bay Books, 1997)

William Price Fox, *Dixiana Moon* (Louisiana State University Press, 2001); *Lunatic Wind: Surviving the Storm of the Century* (Algonquin Books of Chapel Hill, 1992); *Satchel Paige's America* (Fire Ant Books, 2005); and *Wild Blue Yonder* (Crane Hill Publishers, 2002)

Jonathan Franzen, *Farther Away: Essays* (Picador, 2013), and *Freedom* (Picador Reprint Edition, 2011)

Ian Frazier, *Lamentations of the Father: Essays* (Picador, 2009)

G

John Lewis Gaddis, *George F. Kennan: An American Life* (Penguin Books, 2012)

Louis Garans, *Belle-Ile-en-Mer: Histoire d'une Ile* (Palatines Edition, 2012)

Susannah Gardner and **Shane Birley**, *Blogging for Dummies* (For Dummies, 4th edition, 2012)

William Gay, *I Hate to See That Evening Sun Go Down: Collected Stories* (Free Press, 2003)

Leymah Gbowee with **Carol Mithers**, *Mighty Be Our Powers: How Sisterhood, Prayer and Sex Changed a Nation at War* (Beast Books, 2011)

Pamela Gemin, *Another Creature* (University of Arkansas Press, 2010)

Allen Ginsberg, *Collected Poems 1947-1997* (Harper Perennial Modern Classics, 2007)

James Gleick, *Genius: The Life and Science of Richard Feynman* (Vintage, 1993)

Jaimy Gordon, *Lord of Misrule* (McPherson, 2010)

Erica Goss, *Wild Place* (Finishing Line Press, 2012)

Ulysses S. Grant, *Personal Memoirs of Ulysses S. Grant* (Kindle edition, Amazon Digital Services)

Jeff Guinn, *The Last Gunfight: The Real Story of the Shootout at the O.K. Corral—and How It Changed the American West* (Tantor Media, 2012)

Allan Gurganus, *Oldest Living Confederate Widow Tells All* (Vintage, 2001)

H

Joe Haldeman, *The Forever War* (St. Martin's Griffin Reprint Edition, 2009)

Donald Hall, *Eagle Pond* (Mariner Books, 2007)

Thomas Hardy, *Jude the Obscure* (Empire Books, 2012)

Jonathan Harris, *The Wave That Did Not Break (The Ash Tree Poetry)* (Tebot Bach, 2010)

Michael Harris, *The Chieu Hoi Saloon* (PM Press, 2010)

Erica Heller, *Yossarian Slept Here: When Joseph Heller was Dad, the Apthorp Was Home, and Life Was a Catch-22* (Simon and Schuster, 2011)

Lillian Hellman, *The Children's Hour* (Dramatists Play Service, 1953)

Ernest Hemingway, *The Sun Also Rises* (Scribner, 2006)

Kaui Hart Hemmings, *The Descendants* (Random House, 2011)

Dave Hickey, *Air Guitar: Essays on Art & Democracy* (Art Issues Press, 1997)

Joe Hill, *NOS4A2* (William Morrow, 2013)

Jane Hirshfield, *Given Sugar, Given Salt* (1st edition, Harper, 2001)

Christopher Hitchens, "When the King Saved God," *Vanity Fair*, May 2011 [http://www.vanityfair.com/culture/features/2011/05/hitchens-201105]; and *Arguably: Essays* (Twelve, 2012)

Hugh Holman and **William Harmon**, editors, *A Handbook to Literature* (5th ed., Macmillan, 1986)

Gerard Manley Hopkins, *Everyman's Library Pocket Poets* (Knopf, 1995)

Michel Houellebecq, *The Map and the Territory* (Knopf, 2012)

Samuel P. Huntington, *The Clash of Civilizations and the Remaking of World Order* (Touchstone, 1996)

Aldous Huxley, *Brave New World* (Harper Perennial Modern Classics, 2006)

I

Sydney Iaukea, *The Queen and I: A Story of Dispossessions and Reconnections in Hawai'i* (University of California Press, 2011)

John Irving, *The Cider House Rules* (Ballantine, 1993)

Walter Isaacson, *Einstein: His Life and Universe* (Simon and Schuster, 2007)

Aquila Ismail, *Of Martyrs and Marigolds* (Create Space Independent Publishing Platform, 2012)

J

Henry James, *The Turn of the Screw and Other Short Novels* (Signet Classics, 1995)

Derek Jarman, *Chroma: A Book of Color* (University of Minnesota Press, 2010)

James Joyce, *The Portable James Joyce* (Penguin Reprint, 1976)

Heidi Julavits, *The Vanishers, a Novel* (Doubleday, 2012)

K

Franz Kafka, *The Collected Stories,* (Everyman's Library, 1993)

Mary Karr, *Lit: A Memoir (PS)* (Harper Perennial, 2010) and *The Liar's Club: A Memoir* (Penguin Books, 2005)

Philip Kerr, *Berlin Noir* (Penguin, 1993)

Stephen King, *The Shining* (Anchor Reprint, 2012)

Karen Kingston, *Clear Your Clutter with Feng Shui*

(Three Rivers Press, 1999).

Elizabeth Kostova, *The Historian* (Back Bay Books, 2005)

Steve Kowit, *The Dumbbell Nebula* (Roundhouse, 2000)

Hari Kunzru, *Gods Without Men* (Vintage, 2013)

L

Philip Larkin, *Collected Poems*, edited by Anthony Thwaite (Farrar, Straus and Giroux, 2004)

D.H. Lawrence, *Collected Stories: D.H. Lawrence* (Everyman's Library, 1994); *Love Among the Haystacks and Other Stories* (Cambridge University Press, 1987); *Sons and Lovers* (Empire Books, 2011); and *Studies in Classic American Literature* (Shearsman books, 2011)

Deborah Lawrenson, *The Lantern* (Harper, 2011)

Chang-rae Lee, *The Surrendered* (Riverhead Trade, reprint edition, 2011)

David Lehman, editor, *The Oxford Book of American Poetry*, (Oxford University Press, 2006)

Jonah Lehrer, *Imagine: How Creativity Works* (Houghton Mifflin, 2012. Note: then pulled from circulation.)

Elmore Leonard, *Raylan* (William Morrow, 2012)

Alan Lloyd-Smith, *American Gothic Fiction: An Introduction* (Continuum, 2004)

Jack Lopez, *Cholos & Surfers* (Capra Press, 1998)

M

Sarah Maclay, *Music for the Black Room* (University of Tampa Press, 2011)

Beryl Markham, *West With the Night*, (BN Publishing, 2012)

Karl Marlantes, *What It Is Like to Go to War* (Atlantic Montly Press, 2011)

George R.R. Martin *A Clash of Kings*, the second book in the *A Song of Ice and Fire* series (Bantam, 2011)

Robert K. Massie, *Catherine the Great* (Random House, 2012)

Carson McCullers, *The Heart Is a Lonely Hunter* (1st Mariner Books edition, 2004)

David McCullough, *The Greater Journey: Americans in Paris* (Simon and Schuster, 2011)

Ian McEwan, *Amsterdam* (Anchor, 1999); *Saturday* (Anchor, 2006); *In Between the Sheets* (Anchor, 1994); and *The Comfort of Strangers* (Anchor, 1994)

Bill McKibben, *Eaarth: Making a Life on a Tough New Planet* (St. Martin's Griffin, 2011)

Herman Melville, *Bartleby, the Scrivener* (Create Space, 2013)

John Miedema, *Slow Reading* (Litwin Books, 2009)

Joseph Millar, *Overtime* (Eastern Washington University Press, 2001)

Sue Miller, *The Good Mother,* (Harper & Row, 1986)

Czeslaw Milosz, editor, *A Book of Luminous Things: An International Anthology of Poetry* (Mariner Books, reprint edition, 1998) and *The Witness of Poetry* (Harvard U. Press, 1984)

Waddie Mitchell, *Waddie's Whole Load: The Cowboy Poetry of Waddie Mitchell* (Gibbs Smith, 1994)

Karen Moller, *Technicolor Dreamin': The 1960's Rainbow and Beyond* (Trafford Publishing, 2006)

Leigh Montville, *Evel: The High-Flying Life of Evel Knievel: American Showman, Daredevil, and Legend* (Doubleday, 2011)

Christopher Moore, *Sacre Bleu!* (William Morrow Paperbacks, 2012)

Wes Moore, *The Other Wes Moore: One Name, Two Fates* (Spiegel & Grau, 2011)

C.E. Morgan, *All the Living* (Farrar, Straus and Giroux, 2009)

Blake Morrison and **Andrew Motion**, editors, *The Penguin Book of Contemporary British Poetry* (Penguin UK, 1999)

Toni Morrison, *Beloved* (Vintage, 2004)

Kate Moses, *Wintering: A Novel of Sylvia Plath* (Anchor, 2003)

Horacio Castellanos Moya, *Senselessness*, translated by Katherine Silver (New Directions, 2008)

Bill Moyers, *Healing and the Mind* (Main Street Books, 1995)

Therese Mulligan and **Hans-Michael Koetzle,** *Photo Icons: The Story Behind the Pictures* (Taschen, 2005)

Haruki Murakami, *After Dark* (Vintage, 2008); *Wind-Up Bird Chronicle*, translated by Jay Rubin (Vintage, 1998); and *Kafka on the Shore* (Vintage, 2006)

Paul Murray, *Skippy Dies* (Faber & Faber, 2011)

N

Vladimir Nabokov, *Ada or Ardor* (first edition, McGraw-Hill, 1969)

Ann Napolitano, *A Good Hard Look* (Penguin Press HC, 2011)

Pablo Neruda, *The Captain's Verses: Love Poems* (New Directions, 2009)

Jo Nesbo & Don Bartlett, *The Leopard* (Vintage, 2012)

Lynn H. Nicholas, *The Rape of Europa: The Fate of Europe's Treasures in the Third Reich and the Second World War* (Vintage, 1995)

David Nichols, ed., with a foreword by **Studs Terkel**, *Ernie's War: The Best of Ernie Pyle's World War II Dispatches* (Random House, 1986)

O

Joyce Carol Oates, *The Falls* (Harper Perennial, 2005); and, editor, *American Gothic Tales* (Plume, 1996)

Tim O'Brien, *The Things They Carried* (Mariner Books, 2009)

Flannery O'Connor, *Collected Works* (Library of America, 1988)

Eric Olsen and Glenn Schaeffer, *We Wanted to Be Writers* (Skyhorse Publishing, 2011)

P

Anthony Pagden, *Worlds at War: The 2,500-Year Struggle Between East and West* (Random House, 2008)

Abraham Pais, *Subtle Is the Lord: The Science and Life* *of Albert Einstein* (Oxford University Press, 2005)

Chris Pavone, *The Expats* (Broadway, 2013)

Maxwell Perkins and **John Hall Wheelock**, *Editor to Author: The Letters of Maxwell E. Perkins* (Scribners, 1997)

Jayne Anne Phillips, *Lark and Termite* (Vintage, 2010)

Terry Pratchett, *Unseen Academicals* (Harper, 2010); and *Snuff* (Harper, 2012)

Leah Price, *Unpacking My Library: Writers and Their Books* (Yale University Press, 2011)

R

Rebecca Rasmussen, *The Bird Sisters: A Novel* (Broadway Books, 2011)

John Rember, *MFA in a Box: A Why to Write Book* (Dream of Things, 2011)

Laurisa White Reyes, *The Rock of Ivanore* (Tanglewood Press, 2012)

Richard Rhodes, *Hedy's Folly: The Life and Breakthrough Inventions of Hedy Lamarr, the Most Beautiful Woman in the World*, by (Vintage Reprint Edition, 2012)

Keith Richards, *Life* (Hachette Audio, 2010)

Marilynne Robinson, *Gilead* (Picador, 2006); *Home* (Picador, 2009); and *When I Was a Child I read Books* (Picador Reprint Edition, 2013)

Madame Romaine de Lyon, *The Art of Cooking Omelettes* (Doubleday, 1963)

Fran Ross, *Oreo* (Northeastern University Press, 2000)

Lola Ruff, *Called by Name… Called to Serve* (L. Ruff, 2011)

Ann Rule, *The Stranger Beside Me* (Pocketbooks, 2008)

Karen Russell, *Swamplandia!* (Vintage, 2011)

Richard Russo, *That Old Cape Magic* (Vintage, 1st reprint edition, 2010)

S

Tayeb Salih, *Season of Migration to the North* (NYRB Classics, 2009)

James Salter, *The Hunters: A Novel* (Vintage, 1999) and *Light Years* (Vintage, 1995)

Jose Saramago, *Blindness* (Harvest Books, 1999)

George Saunders, *In Persuasion Nation* (Riverhead Trade, 2007)

Simon Schama, *Citizens: A Chronicle of the French Revolution* (Vintage, 1990)

Elizabeth Hun Schmidt, ed., *The Poets Laureate Anthology* (W.W. Norton, 2010)

Audrey Schulman, *Three Weeks in December* (Europa Editions, 2012)

Arnold Schwarzenegger with **Peter Petre**, *Total Recall: My Unbelievably True Life Story* (Simon and Schuster, 2012)

David Sedaris, *Naked* (Back Bay Books, 1998)

Lucius Shepard, *The Jaguar Hunter* (Four Walls Eight Windows, 2001)

Charles J. Shields, *And So It Goes: Kurt Vonnegut: A Life* (St. Martin's Griffin, 2012)

Julia Flynn Siler, *Lost Kingdom: Hawaii's Last Queen, the Sugar Kings, and America's First Imperial Adventure* (Grove Press, 2013)

Charles Simic, *Selected Poems 1963-2003* (Faber, 2004)

Rebecca Skloot, *The Immortal Life of Henrietta Lacks* (Broadway, 2011)

Jane Smiley, *Private Life* (Knopf, 2010); *Moo* (Anchor, 2009); *13 Ways of Looking at the Novel* (Anchor, 2006); *Greenlanders* (Anchor, 2005); *A Thousand Acres* (Anchor, 2003); *Charles Dickens* (Viking, 2002); and *Horse Heaven* (Ballantine, 2001)

Cynthia Leitich Smith, *Diabolical* (Candlewick, 2013)

Patti Smith, *Just Kids* (Harper Collins e-books, 2010)

Zadie Smith, *On Beauty* (Penguin Books, 2006)

Blake Snyder, *Save the Cat Goes to the Movies: The Screenwriter's Guide to Every Story Ever Told* (Michael Wiese Productions, 2007)

Scott Spencer, *Man in the Woods* (Ecco, 2010)

Dana Spiotta, *Stone Arabia* (Scribner, 2012)

Edward St. Aubyn, *At Last* (Picador, 2012)

David St. John, *Study For The World's Body: New and Selected Poems* (Perennial, 1994)

Jonathan Stedall, *Where on Earth is Heaven?* (Floris Books, 2009)

Kathryn Stockett, *The Help* (Berkley Trade, 2011)

Rex Stout, *Triple Jeopardy: A Nero Wolfe Threesome* (Bantam, 1992)

Cheryl Strayed, *Wild: From Lost to Found on the Pacific*

Crest Trail (Knopf, 2012)

William Styron, *Lie Down in Darkness* (Vintage, 1992)

John Jeremiah Sullivan, *Pulphead: Essays* (Farrar, Straus and Giroux Originals, 2011) and *Blood Horses: Notes of a Sportswriter's Son* (Farrar, Straus and Giroux, 2004)

John Szarkowski, *Looking at Photographs: 100 Pictures from the Collection of the Museum of Modern Art* (Museum of Modern Art, 1976)

T

Kono Taeko, *Toddler-Hunting & Other Stories*, translated by Lucy North (New Directions, 1996)

Paco Ignacio Taibo II,*'68* (Seven Stories Press, 2004)

Johan Theorin, *The Darkest Room* (Delta, 2009)

Ngugi wa Thiong'o, *A Grain of Wheat* (Penguin Classics, 2012)

Henry David Thoreau, *Faith in a Seed* (Island Press, 1993)

Alexis de Tocqueville, *The Old Regime and the Revolution* (Anchor, 1955)

Charles Todd, *The Confession* (William Morrow, 2012)

Leo Tolstoy, *The Death of Ivan Ilyich and Other Stories* (Vintage Classics, 2010)

V

N.I. Vavilov, *Five Continents* (International Plant Genetics Research Institute, 1997)

Helen Vendler, *Dickinson: Selected Poems and Commentaries* (Belknap Press, 2012)

William T. Vollmann, *The Rainbow Stories* by (Penguin Books, reprint edition, 1992)

W

Fred Waitzkin, *The Dream Merchant* (Thomas Dunne Books (2013)

Claire Vaye Watkins, *Battleborn* (Riverhead, 2013)

James D. Watson, *The Double Helix: A Personal Account of the Discovery of the Structure of DNA* (Touchstone, 2011)

Tim Weiner, *Enemies: A History of the FBI* (Random House Trade Paperbacks, 2013) and *Legacy of Ashes: The History of the CIA* (Anchor Reprint Edition, 2008)

Edith Wharton, everything, including *The Age of Innocence* (Dover, 1997) and *The Buccaneers* (Penguin Reprint Edition, 1994), with an ending written by Marion Mainwaring, as Wharton died before finishing the novel.

Oscar Wilde, *The Portable Oscar Wilde*, edited by Richard Aldington and Stanley Weintraub (Penguin, 1981)

Laura Ingalls Wilder, *Little House Collection* (HarperCollins, 2004)

Tobias Wolff, ed., *The Vintage Book of Contemporary American Short Stories* (Vintage, 1994)

Y

Richard Yates, *Revolutionary Road* (Vintage, 2000)

John Yount, *The Trapper's Last Shot* (Random House, 1973)

Z

J. Peder Zane, *The Top Ten: Writers Pick Their Favorite Books* (W.W. Norton & Company, 2007)

Howard Zinn, *A People's History of the United States* (Harper Perennial Modern Classics, 2005)

William Zinsser, *Writing About Your Life: A Journey Into the Past* (De Capo Press, 2005) and *On Writing Well: 30th Anniversary Edition* (Harper Perennial, 2006)

Emile Zola, *The Earth* (The Emile Zola Society, 2011); *Nana* (Penguin Classics, 1972); and *The Belly of Paris* (Oxford University Press, 2009)

About the Editors

Eric and Cheryl Olsen are a husband and wife writing/ editing team. Both graduates of the University of Iowa Writers' Workshop, they are proficient book hoarders who have managed to fill closets, a basement, and all available bookshelves—especially the ones by the bed—with specimens from every literary genre. This volume is a natural extension of that proclivity, in no way intended to help bibliophiles with their addiction.

More complete bios can be found here
http://wewantedtobewriters.com/our-authors/eric-olsen/
and here
http://wewantedtobewriters.com/our-authors/cheryl-olsen/

www.ingramcontent.com/pod-product-compliance
Lightning Source LLC
Chambersburg PA
CBHW070333120726
47909CB00008B/2686

* 9 7 8 0 9 7 9 5 8 9 8 7 4 *